GREAT AMERICAN MYSTERIES

Other books by Randall Floyd
from August House Publishers

Great Southern Mysteries

Bigfoot, water witches, the Carolina Bays,
the Biloxi mermaid, and other enduring mysteries
of the Deep South.

More Great Southern Mysteries

Florida's fountain of youth, ghosts of the Alamo,
lost maidens of the Okefenokee, terror on the Natchez Trace,
and other mystifying stories from the American South.

GREAT AMERICAN MYSTERIES

Raining snakes, fabled cities of gold, strange disappearances, and other baffling tales.

E. RANDALL FLOYD

August House Publishers, Inc.

LITTLE ROCK

Published by August House, Inc.,
P.O. Box 3223, Little Rock, Arkansas, 72203,
501-372-5450.

Printed in the United States of America

10 9 8 7 6 5 4 3

LIBRARY OF CONGRESS CATALOGING-IN-PUBLICATION DATA

Floyd, E. Randall
Great American Mysteries / E. Randall Floyd — 1st ed.
p.   cm.
Includes bibliographical references.
ISBN 0-87483-171-7 (acid free) : $18.95
ISBN 0-87483-170-9 (pb: acid free) : $9.95
1. Curiosities and wonders—United States—Anecdotes. 2. United
States—History, Local—Anecdotes I. Title

E179.F66   1991
001.9'4'0973—dc20   91-6566

Executive: Ted Parkhurst
Project editor: Judith Faust
Design director: Ted Parkhurst
Cover design: Byron Taylor
Typography: Lettergraphics Little Rock

This book is printed on archival-quality paper which meets the
guidelines for performance and durability of the Committee on
Production Guidelines for Book Longevity of the
Council on Library Resources.

AUGUST HOUSE, INC.   PUBLISHERS   LITTLE ROCK

In memory of
Albert "Bo" Fendig, Jr.
a lover of nature
and a great storyteller

Preface

A famous poet said that people who make history leave "footprints on the sands of time." But as the centuries roll by and the winds of change blow away the footprints, what remains of their passing?

Legends, of course. Legends that keep alive the glories and deeds and immutable dreams of those who came before. Without legends, would we have sought Troy or Tutankhamen's tomb? Known of Agamemnon or Babylon's hanging gardens? Gone to the New World? Long ago we realized that the written word is not reliable—that the record of past events is sometimes garbled, distorted, edited to conform to standards of the time. All too often, the records have completely disappeared, leaving us with only dreamlike tatters of truth.

That which we don't understand or can't explain becomes a mystery. The past is full of mysteries—mysteries locked away in desert tombs and lost in dark forests, scattered on far mountain tops and beneath storm-tossed waves. The present has its mysteries, too—UFOs, the Bermuda Triangle, Bridey Murphy, and Bigfoot. Our romantic fascination for them persists in spite of ridiculous supermarket tabloids, regurgitated "docudramas," and an academic community reluctant to consider that somewhere behind all the hysteria must lurk a bit of truth.

Try as it may, science can never solve all the great mysteries of the world. And that's probably just as well. Who'd want to live in a world without mysteries, anyway?

Why are Americans so enthralled by mysteries? The question is often asked and rightfully so. Surely the answer must lie in the mists of our primordial past, back when a dark cave was not only a snug, safe shelter but also the center of a most uncertain universe. Can you imagine what wonder and terror our ancestors must have felt as they crouched around the flickering embers of a fire, gazing out into the darkness just beyond the cave's yawning mouth?

We seem born with an insatiable curiosity about the unknown. It's the same curiosity that led Heinrich Schliemann on his relentless quest to find ancient Troy and Agamemnon's grave. It drove Sir Arthur Evans to Crete, made Howard Carter keep digging until he stood trembling in the brooding darkness of Tutankhamen's tomb, forced Christopher Columbus across the legend-haunted sea.

Even today, while rockets hurtle through space and computerized technology unlocks many of life's most guarded secrets, the world is yet full of mysteries and wonder. Everywhere we turn, there are riddles of nature and science, and baffling phenomena that seem more supernatural than natural—an endless stream of strange events that touch and shape our everyday lives.

My purpose in writing this book is to offer you brief tellings of some of *this* country's greatest unexplained mysteries. Certainly no one book of fewer than two hundred pages could possibly hope to cover them all.

So, for this volume—the first in a planned series—I've selected the tales that I feel are especially compelling. The details about each presented here are not intended to be complete. They come to you in brief and concise form, much as they might be found in a newspaper—but without, I hope, sacrificing any of the essential elements, drama, and color of each.

They date from the first appearances of man, up through the arrival of Renaissance Europeans, the Colonial era, and on into modern times. (If you're interested in learning more about each topic, I recommend that you consult the bibliography at the back of the book.)

Many of these narratives are based on legends and myths. But, as a wise man once implied—indeed, only a few paragraphs ago—behind every legend is at least a bit of truth.

So, read and enjoy. Let your mind wander with Amelia Earhart on her final flight across the Pacific. Climb rugged Mount Shasta, where strange white-robed survivors of an ancient civilization once practiced midnight rituals. Come face-to-face—or face-to-chest—with Bigfoot in the misty wilds of the Pacific Northwest. Relive the bewildering saga of Bridey Murphy.

It's all here—the mystery, the enchantment, the enduring romance. Welcome to my favorite great American mysteries.

E. Randall Floyd
Augusta, Georgia
1990

Contents

In the Midst of Life

Into the Unknown

In the Realm of Spirits

Unearthly Incursions

Bibliography   183

Index of Place Names   188

Notorious Acts

Entertaining Satan
in New England

IN THE SPRING OF 1692, several young girls in a rural New England village began to speak in strange tongues, suffer terrifying hallucinations, and throw themselves to the floor in grotesque fits of passion.

They foamed at the mouth and displayed other equally alarming symptoms—bizarre bodily contortions, loss of memory and appetite, choking sensations at the throat. Worst of all, they complained of being bitten and pinched by unseen specters who tormented them in a variety of ingenious and cruel ways.

Doctors who examined the afflicted girls found no physical cause for their mysterious ailments. Except for a few marks where the patients claimed to have been abused by "invisible tormentors," their skin was unblemished, and they appeared in excellent health.

When the symptoms did not go away after a few days, the stepfather of one of the girls—a stern Puritan minister named Samuel Parris—concluded that witchcraft was behind the trouble. In desperation, he called upon the clergy-dominated court system to help rid the town of its "evil hand."

So began the infamous witch trials of Salem Village, Massachusetts. The trials, which lasted for several months and resulted in the imprisonment of hundreds of men, women, and children and the deaths of at least twenty, are arguably the most notorious in the history of superstitious practice in the New World.

By the time the horror had passed, reputations had been ruined, fortunes lost, and an entire social order turned upside down.

The trouble had begun innocently enough at the Reverend Parris's own house. It was there in the shuttered gloom of the kitchen that a West Indian slave named Tituba enthralled the bored teenage girls with bewitching tales of demonic possession and sorcery. Even though subsequent events were related to European rather than Afro-Caribbean occult tradition, Tituba's hair-raising stories provided the girls with enough fodder to concoct their own macabre brand of madness.

When Parris walked into the kitchen unexpectedly he knew something was wrong. Young girls surely don't writhe and convulse on the floor or squeal and crow and mew like barnyard animals unless some bewitching spell has been put upon them.

He recognized the signs instantly—witchcraft!

It didn't take long for news of the strange events at the Parris household to spread throughout the village. Soon other children started throwing fits and wild tantrums, all the while accusing unseen tormentors of making them bark and mew like animals. Within days "witch fever" had spread to nearby villages and as far away as Boston.

Compared to the persecutions sweeping Europe at the time, the hysteria manifested in Salem was insignificant. But it was here amid the deep forests and lonely stone farmhouses of colonial Massachusetts that the proceedings were so well documented and the injustices so flagrant that they continue to stir controversy even today.

It should be noted that Salem—now called Danvers—was not the first place to experience trouble with witches in New England. The first person on record to be tried and convicted for being a witch was Mrs. Anne Hibbins, widow of a wealthy Boston merchant. In 1656, she went to the gallows for allegedly having consorted with the devil and his familiars.

Other cases followed, first in 1662, then in 1663, and another in 1682. The pattern was always the same—someone, perhaps a neighbor or business associate, would inform authorities that the accused victim had convulsed or otherwise acted strangely, and arrest and trial would follow. Not all convicted suspects were hanged; a few were drowned. Others were stoned or burned alive.

When a Grand Court convened in Salem to investigate local charges of witchcraft, Abigail Williams, Ann Putnam, and Betty Parris identified Tituba and two other local women—Sarah Good and Sarah Osburne—as having "tormented and hurt them in spectral form." All three women were hauled to jail to await sentencing.

Meanwhile, Ann Putnam and Abigail Williams were busily pointing out other tormentors. There seemed no pattern to their indiscriminate accusations, as victim after victim was herded into the packed courtroom to stand trembling before his or her wild-eyed young prosecutors. Each time, the girls would fall to the floor in fits, shrieking and wailing and twitching like animals as "the devil" sought control of their souls.

The first "witch" to die on Gallows Hill—later renamed Witches' Hill—was a poor, gaudily attired tavern keeper named Bridget Bishop, who had been suspected of witchcraft in the past. That was June 10. By the end of the year, an estimated two hundred other persons would be arrested in Salem Village alone on charges of witchcraft, of whom eighteen would be hanged and another pressed to death beneath heavy stones.

Suspects brought up on charges included at least one minister, several pious churchgoers, a police officer, and several small children. Besides those executed, two died in jail, one was held indefinitely in jail without trial, two women pleaded pregnancy and survived long enough to be reprieved, one escaped from jail, and five made confessions that resulted in their freedom.

"Confessions" were serious business in Salem. Only those who admitted to their dealings with Satan had any hope of escaping the hangman's rope; those who refused to confess were submitted to brutal torture tests that invariably ended in their deaths, and thus their convictions, anyway. One woman, Mary Easty, who protested the charges against her condemned sister was herself accused of being a witch and promptly hanged.

Those who dared come forward to demand an end to the madness were treated likewise. When the deputy constable at Salem Village, a well-liked man named John Willard, refused to hang any more victims, he was hauled into court where the girls quickly identified him, too, as one of their tormentors. Willard was hanged.

A similar fate befell the Reverend George Burroughs, a former minister from Salem. Based of the testimony of Ann Putnam and Mercy Lewis, Burroughs was convicted of having celebrated midnight feasts and "unholy communions" with broomstick-riding witches and the devil in a field behind his house.

The fact that Burroughs was eighty miles away on the night he allegedly entertained his demonic visitors did not sway Cotton Mather, the overzealous witch hunter and presiding official at the trial. On August 19, the Reverend Burroughs was led up to the gallows on Witches' Hill. Though he calmly recited the Lord's Prayer over and over—a feat it was said no witch could do—the black-hooded executioner placed the noose around his neck and kicked open the trapdoor.

Eventually, interest in the witch trials began to wane. The final gasp came when Abigail Williams and her friends pointed the guilty finger toward none other than the wife of Governor William Phips himself. Phips, who was also president of Harvard University, reacted swiftly. In a rage, he suspended the special commission investigating witchcraft and ordered that all suspects being held in prison be released.

The Salem witch trials were over.

As soon as the governor's proclamation was announced, dozens of prosecutors, judges, and other investigators stepped forward and quickly admitted that they had erred. On January 14, 1696, the members of the jury published their "Confession of Error," in which they stated that they had unwittingly been "prevailed with to take up such evidence against the accused, as on further consideration and better information we justly fear was insufficient for the touching of the lives of any...We do therefore hereby signify to all in general and to the surviving sufferers in especial, our deep sense of and sorrow for our errors...we justly fear that we were sadly deluded and mistaken..."

The final irony came in 1706 when several of the girls admitted they had acted out their demonic torment "for sport."

"I desire to lie in the dust and be humbled for it, in that I was a cause, with others, of so sad a calamity," Ann Putnam said in a confession read in Salem Church.

And what about Tituba, the old slave woman who had helped start it all? After the remaining survivors of the horror were freed from jail and pardoned, she was confiscated and sold to defray the costs of the trial.

As far as anyone can tell, Tituba spent her remaining days on earth enthralling other youngsters with the mysterious arts of her ancestral homeland.

Frontier Cannibal
of the Rockies

HAD THEY NOT BEEN SO greedy, perhaps the small band of prospectors working a claim on the western slopes of the Rockies would have been sensible and left when the first snow fell that winter of 1874.

It must have been an insatiable hunger for gold that kept them on their claim, unwilling to budge even as savage winds ripped down from the mountains and snowdrifts five feet high began piling up around their camp in the San Juan range near Lake City, Colorado.

Later, when some of the men finally decided to make a desperate run for it, it was too late. They were trapped. Even worse, a full-scale blizzard had set in—and food supplies were running dangerously low.

The storm that struck Colorado that winter was one of the hardest in history. Entire towns scattered among the higher elevations were shut off from the outside world. Roads disappeared. Rivers and lakes froze. For weeks, not a wagon rolled west of Denver or Colorado Springs; it would be months before even some of the lower passes opened.

No one knows how many people stranded in the high country died that year. The situation must have seemed particularly grim for the party of half-starved miners clinging to life in the rugged San Juan Mountains. Snowbound and out of food, they were sure to freeze or starve long before help could arrive.

What happened next remains one of Colorado's greatest unsolved mysteries. According to the only survivor of the group, a grizzled Union Army veteran named Alferd Packer, the men were on the verge of starvation when he volunteered to take the rifle and go hunt for food. When he returned empty-handed five days later, Packer said he found four of his fellow miners dead—hacked to death with an axe.

The fifth miner, still very much alive but crazed with hunger, charged him with an axe the moment he stepped foot inside camp. Packer said he had no choice but to shoot his attacker, Shannon Wilson Bell, in self-defense. On the verge of starvation himself, Packer later admitted, he cannibalized Bell's remains by stripping away the flesh with a knife.

When authorities finally reached the surviving prospector, they found a grisly scene—human remains boiling in a stewpot, severed arms and legs and dismembered skeletons of the dead five miners strewn about the campsite.

Packer was arrested on the spot and charged with the murder of his companions. Within a few days, he escaped, and was recaptured nine years later. At his trial in Denver, he swore that he had killed only Bell, and him in self-defense. As for the fate of the other miners, Packer theorized Bell had killed them all with the same axe he had attacked Packer with.

When charges of cannibalism were raised, Packer admitted to having eaten Bell. He claimed it was Bell who had killed then consumed portions of his companions while he was off hunting.

The jury refused to believe Packer's incredible story. He was found guilty on five counts of manslaughter—not cannibalism—and sentenced to forty years in prison. Paroled in 1901, he settled in a small town south of Denver, where he died six years later.

For years following the hideous ordeal in the mountains, controversy stalked Packer's memory. Many people believed the miner's bizarre story, but there were others who weren't so sure. Scholars researching Packer's background managed to put together an unpleasant scenario that tended to support those who thought him guilty; Packer, they said, was a notorious liar and a petty thief who had been disciplined while serving in the Army during the Civil War for "plundering" his fellow soldiers.

In 1989, a team of experts led by James E. Starrs, professor of law and forensic science at George Washington University, traveled to the scene of the carnage and there unearthed the skeletons of the miners. Armed with sophisticated equipment, Starrs found what he considered conclusive proof that it had, indeed, been Packer who butchered and ate his companions.

"It is plain as a pikestaff that Packer was the one who was on the attack, not Bell," Starrs said, explaining that wounds on the bones of three of the victims "were caused by a hatchet-like instrument at a time when these persons were defending themselves from the attack of an aggressor." The marks, the professor pointed out, suggested the victims had raised their arms to fend off a rain of blows from an axe.

Starrs said the angle of the blade marks on the bones from which the flesh had been taken—including the bones believed to be Bell's—indicated that the cuts were all made by the same person—in all probability, Packer.

Nonsense, retorted Starrs' critics, who claimed there was no way scientifically to substantiate such a finding. Anthropologist Walter H. Birkby of the Arizona State Museum said a study he recently conducted actually supported Packer's story.

In time, bizarre accounts of Packer and death and survival in the wilds of the Rocky Mountains grew into legend. Hundreds of newspaper and magazine stories and at least one television documentary have examined the case seeking to unravel the mystery.

Whatever his crime, the notorious "frontier cannibal" has been a fixture in Colorado folk history since the turn of the century. His bust was even displayed for a while in the state capitol.

In Lake City, a bar owner is credited with the tale that the local sentencing judge reportedly said to Packer: "There was sivin Dimicrats in Hinsdale County, and you et five of them, God damn ye!"

In 1968, a student protest over the quality of food in a University of Colorado dining hall ended with the facility being renamed after Packer. Since then, the university has observed Alferd Packer Day every April, with a parade and a "speed-eating contest" featuring barbecued ribs and steak.

The letterhead of the Alferd Packer Society of Washington, D.C., one of several around the country, reads: "Serving Our Fellow Man Since 1874." The National Press Club in Washington has an Alferd Packer Memorial Grill.

In case you've wondered, one small related mystery was cleared up when Duane J. Dillon, a criminal investigator from Martinez, California, concluded that Packer spelled his first name Alferd, not Alfred. He said official records show the name as "Alfred," but that when Packer signed documents, he used "Alferd."

"Lizzie Borden
Took an Axe..."

SHORTLY BEFORE NOON ON August 4, 1892, Andrew Borden, a successful undertaker in the small town of Fall River, Massachusetts, quietly closed his office, hopped into his buggy and drove home for lunch.

He didn't intend to stay long—just to grab a catnap and quick bite before going back to work. Though he had retired some months back, he still kept tabs on things down at the parlor; you never knew who might show up.

Waiting for him at home was his Irish housekeeper, twenty-six year-old Bridget Sullivan, who had been with the Borden family for nearly three years. Ordinarily his wife, Abby, would have greeted him at the door, but for some reason she was nowhere to be found when Andrew arrived.

In customary fashion, Andrew told Bridget what he wanted for lunch, then settled down on the sofa for his nap. From the kitchen, Bridget heard Lizzie, Borden's youngest daughter, descend the stairway into the living room where her father lay.

Lizzie, thirty-two, was unmarried and still lived at home. Bubbly one moment, moody the next, Lizzie was a hard-working member of the Central Congregational Church where she taught Sunday School and helped out with a variety of other church activities. Not one to be idle, Lizzie also was active in the Ladies' Fruit and Flower Mission, the

Woman's Christian Temperance Union, and the Good Samaritan Charity Hospital.

Even though the red-haired spinster was well liked and respected in the community, she despised her own homelife. She quarreled openly with her older sister, Emma, also single and living at home, as well as with her stepmother, Abby, only six years her senior.

Andrew Borden apparently doted on his younger daughter, lavishing on her expensive gifts—a diamond ring, a sealskin cape, even a grand tour of Europe once. Lizzie worshipped her father in return, although she often begged him to move the family to a bigger, more modern home "on the hill," in Fall River's most fashionable neighborhood.

The house was hot and silent that day as Andrew Borden lay dozing on the sofa. Seeking to draw in a fresh breeze from the back porch, Bridget quietly opened the back door, humming as she prepared Mr. Andrew's meal. The stout Irishwoman didn't care much for Miss Lizzie. She wondered what on earth she was up to out there in the living room—usually she'd be in the kitchen helping prepare her father's lunch.

A few minutes later Lizzie appeared in the doorway, visibly shaken. "Come down quick," she said. "Father's dead; somebody came in and killed him."

Bridget dropped the plate of sandwiches she was holding and raced toward the living room, Lizzie trailing closely behind. She wasn't prepared for what she saw on the sofa—it was the most horrible thing she'd ever seen in her life.

Mr. Andrew was dead, all right. His face was a bloody mess, hacked so badly she hardly recognized him. Half of an eye hung from its socket. One ear trailed from the side of his head, suspended on a long string of flesh. Though no murder weapon was nearby, such butchery could only have been accomplished by an axe. In fact, investigators later testified that it had been a single axe blow that had killed the old man; nine others had been laid on apparently for good measure.

Moments later the police arrived. Sobbing, but very much in control, Bridget and a neighbor ventured upstairs to fetch a sheet to cover the battered remains of her former employer. It was there, sprawled on the hallway floor in a bloody mass, they discovered Abby Borden, her head nearly severed from her body.

Later, when investigators sat down to put the gruesome pieces of the massacre together, someone remarked how odd it was that Lizzie Borden had not shed a tear throughout the whole ordeal—how she had remained stunningly calm, even as the bloodied bodies of her parents were carted off to the mortuary.

Next day, details about the gruesome double homicide swept across town. Newspapers as far away as New York and Philadelphia carried front page stories about the "crime of the century," demanding that local law enforcement officials bring swiftly to justice the "monster responsible for this black murder."

A local reporter recalled that "the cry of murder swept through the city like a typhoon...murder committed under the very glare of the midday sun within three minutes walk of the City Hall..."

The police were stumped. Not only was there no suspect in custody, the murder weapon was nowhere to be found. It was as if the killer had sneaked into the house in broad daylight, committed the foul deeds, and escaped—all within earshot of the cook. Equally disturbing was the fact that nothing in the house was missing, thereby ruling out robbery as a motive.

Then why—if not for money or jewelry—had two of Fall River's leading citizens been brutally murdered?

All eyes turned toward Bridget, the young Irish maid. But on Saturday, the day of the funerals, police arrested Lizzie. She alone, they theorized, had had the opportunity to kill her parents. The chance of a conviction, though, seemed as remote as the moon.

At her trial, Lizzie gave a bewildering array of conflicting stories about her whereabouts during the murder. At first she said she was "in the back yard." Later she said she was "in the loft getting a piece of iron for sinkers." To another inter-rogator she said, "I was up in the loft eating pears."

Still, if she had been the one swinging the axe that awful day, no one understood how it was that she appeared so neat and clean when the police arrived. Surely, they reasoned, her clothes and hands and hair would have been splattered with the victims' blood.

And the murder weapon—where was the murder weapon?

A few days later an inspector rummaging through the Borden tool shed out back found a freshly cleaned axe head. Could this have been the cruel device that ended the lives of Abby and Andrew Borden? The fact that the wooden handle, from which it would have been difficult to remove bloodstains, was missing convinced investigators that this was, indeed, the weapon.

Then new evidence was introduced that further dam-aged Lizzie's defense. Upon request, she had turned over to police a spotlessly clean, fancy, blue bengaline dress she swore she had worn on the day of the murders. That story seemed unlikely, however; no one wore party dresses of bengaline, a heavy corded cloth, around the house in the August heat.

Confounding the problem was testimony provided by a neighbor, Alice Russell, who reluctantly admitted she had seen Lizzie burn a blue cotton dress in the kitchen stove three days after the murders. The dress, Lizzie explained, had been soiled with brown paint—a color, noted the prosecutor, not unlike that of dried blood.

But an outraged press, supported by the public, rallied behind the frail, soft-spoken woman. How could anyone, the editorials wanted to know, accuse this "innocent and loving and devoted daughter" of such heinous crimes without feel-ing ashamed of themselves? After all, this was the height of the late Victorian age, a time when the gentleness, physical frailty, and docility of the well-bred American woman was the cornerstone of society.

New Englanders were certain that well-brought-up Christian daughters like Lizzie Borden could not possibly commit murder with a hatchet on sunny summer mornings. In those days, women were thought to possess more "natural refinements," "diviner instincts," and stronger "spiritual sensibilities" than men. Proper women were inherently more gentle and truthful than their male counterparts. These were hardly the virtues of an axe murderer.

Overlooked in the public outcry over Lizzie's arrest and trial was the fact she stood to inherit a fortune of several hundred thousand dollars. Also, nobody brought up the fact that Lizzie had often feuded with Abby Borden and even with her father because he repeatedly spurned her request to purchase a new home.

In the end, the jury returned with the only verdict possible under the circumstances: "not guilty." The judge, who had admonished the jurymen to remember that such "a woman of refinement and gentle training... could [not] have conceived and executed so bloody a butchery," seemed genuinely pleased at the decision.

A few years before her death, Lizzie Borden moved to Maplecroft, the neighborhood she had begged her father to move the family to years before. In her final days, she undoubtedly had occasion to hear the nasty rhyme so often sung by schoolchildren to the tune of "Ta-Ra-Ra-Boom-De-Ay!":

> *Lizzie Borden took an axe*
> *And gave her mother forty whacks;*
> *When she saw what she had done,*
> *She gave her father forty-one!*

On June 1, 1927, she died at the age of sixty-six and was buried alongside her stepmother and father in Oak Grove Cemetery. Beneath the imposing monument bearing the Borden name is also buried the truth of one of the greatest American murder mysteries of all time.

Unearthly Incursions

America's Ancient Founding Fathers

WHEN THE FIRST COLONIAL settlers arrived in New England in the 17th century, they were startled to find hundreds of stone buildings dotting the landscape, some of them surrounded by standing stones that resembled the megalithic structures of Europe and North Africa.

The fact that many were covered by huge earthen mounds and capped with large, old oak trees led observers to conclude that the enigmatic stone assemblies were of ancient origin. Some believed they might be older even than the pyramids of Egypt.

In those days it was assumed that a vanished race of Indians had built the structures, since none of the local tribesmen had any knowledge of their construction. Just who those ancient builders were and where they went was anybody's guess. Few settlers had the time or desire to ponder such questions; if they were to survive in this harsh new world, they had work to do.

It didn't take them long, however, to start putting the structures to good use—first as storage cellars for their root crops, then later as centers for illicit whiskey operations. Runaway slaves also used some of the underground dwellings for hideouts.

In time, many of the buildings were dismantled and their ancient stones hauled off to use in dry walls and foundations for houses. By 1853, at least forty percent of the stone structures were either destroyed or severely damaged by building contractors who used the stones for dams and bridges.

One of the largest complexes of stone and slab structures is located near North Salem, New Hampshire. Known as Mystery Hill, this curious configuration of rock buildings and underground chambers is one of America's most baffling archaeological oddities.

A popular tourist attraction, the site consists of an elaborate grouping of twenty-two stone-walled formations, some with roof slabs weighing several tons. Others, sunk deep into the ground, contain high-arching underground vaults.

Since its discovery more than a century ago, historians and archaeologists have pondered the origins of Mystery Hill. Some scholars believe seafaring peoples from Europe or perhaps northern Africa built the brooding rock assemblies thousands of years ago. Others believe the Vikings had a hand in their construction, while one group insists the Indians built it themselves.

In some ways, Mystery Hill resembles Stonehenge and other ancient astronomical observatories of Bronze Age Europe. Sprawling over twenty acres, the elaborate maze is oriented so that the sun sets behind particular standing stones on the days of the equinoxes and the summer and winter solstices.

Some scholars who have studied the ruins point to evidence of more sinister activity. A runnel, or drainage groove, carved into the rectangular surface of one stone altar suggests it may once have been used for human sacrifice. Similar altars found in Portugal and elsewhere in Iberia have long been associated with burial mounds and sacrificial rituals.

In the 1930s, one popular explanation was that a group of shipwrecked Irish monks had built the Mystery Hill complex hundreds of years ago. That didn't explain the stone altar, of course; what use would Irish churchmen have had with such a pagan instrument of worship?

In time, theorists turned to other possibilities. One popular notion was that ancient Israelites—the "ten lost tribes" of the Bible—had masterminded the impressive project. When the theorists needed proof, they found it in the languages of various local Indian tribes—words and phrases that were too similar in meaning and phonetics to the language of the Israelites to be merely coincidental.

Few archaeologists accepted the fanciful theories of the time, preferring to link the origin of the enigmatic stones to native Americans themselves. Some even suggested early settlers were responsible for the stone structures, and all records had been lost over the passage of time.

Beginning in 1967, however, a series of radiocarbon studies on samples of charcoal obtained at Mystery Hill indicated that the site may be at least four thousand years old—too old, say some scholars, to have been built by a technologically backward race of people like the Indians. Mystery Hill, they argued, was surely constructed by some wayward group of ancient mariners, perhaps from Iberia or even Egypt.

One expert who is convinced of a transatlantic connection is Barry Fell, a retired professor of biology from Harvard University. Fell, an energetic New Zealander, has spent the past two decades of his life studying the riddle of Mystery Hill and other megalithic stone structures in New England.

In his bestselling book *America B.C.*, Fell offers what he considers authoritative archaeological and linguistic evidence that about three thousand years ago, roving bands of Celtic mariners crossed the Atlantic from Portugal and Spain and established settlements not only in New England, but as far west as Ohio and Oklahoma.

These Celts, Fell argues, were followed or accompanied by succeeding waves of colonists from Europe and North Africa, many of them speaking Basque, Phoenician and Libyan. The truth, says the hard-digging, fast-talking professor is only now coming to light in the wake of new archaeological excavations in New England.

"Ancient history is inscribed upon the bedrock and buried stone buildings of America," Fell wrote, adding that "the only hands that could have inscribed it were those of ancient people."

Fell, who now makes his home in San Francisco, further maintains that "America...is a treasure house of records of man's achievement upon the high seas in bygone ages. Even more so are our inscribed rocks and tablets a heritage from a forgotten era of colonization. They tell us of settlers who came from the Old World and who remained to become founding fathers of some of the Amerindian nations."

Based on badly eroded inscriptions in the stones, Fell and a handful of other scholars believe that at least some of the stone chambers at Mystery Hill were dedicated to the Phoenician god *Baal*.

"The probability is that other chambers on Mystery Hill were dedicated to other divinities, and that the whole complex was a religious center and astronomical observatory," Fell said.

Barry Fell's findings triggered a storm of controversy when they were published a few years ago. But the scientist, who holds advanced degrees in biology, oceanography, epigraphy, and Celtic language and literature, clings fast to his theories about ancient trans-Atlantic voyages to and from the New World.

"There is more to America's past than appears upon the surface," he said. "A strange unrest is apparent among many of the younger historians and archaeologists...a sense that somehow a very large slice of America's past has mysteriously vanished from our public records."

How else, he asked, "can we explain the ever-swelling tally of puzzling ancient inscriptions now being reported from nearly all parts of the United States, Canada, and Latin America?"

Inscriptions at Mystery Hill and elsewhere in the New World do appear to be written in various European and Mediterranean languages in alphabets that are very old. If Fell's theory is correct, they speak not only of visits by ancient ships, but also of permanent colonies of Celts, Basques, Libyans, and even Egyptians.

The consequences of these discoveries for history and archaeology are immeasurable. As one historian, Professor Norman Totten, has pointed out, it means that thousands of years of American prehistory must now be transferred to history.

"History begins when writing begins, and we now have the oldest written documents of our nation, and the names of the men who wrote them," Totten said.

The Seven Cities of Cibola

IN THE EARLY 16TH CENTURY, one burning dream kept pushing Spanish explorers northward into the wild, uncharted lands beyond Mexico: gold.

Legends about fabulously rich kingdoms where "the streets were paved with gold and the doors of lofty houses studded with precious gems" drove these restless adventurers onward, braving hostile Indians, scorching desert plains, and snow-covered mountain passes.

No one, of course, had any real idea of what lay beyond New Spain. Were there more deserts and mountains, or was it a fruitful land, perhaps an entirely new continent or an endless ocean?

In the grip of gold fever, a wishful fantasy was born in the minds of the dashing conquistadores—why not palaces and temples? Cities of gold just as the legends promised? One and all, these men were prepared to risk everything to find those mysterious glittering realms.

The most popular legend at the time was that of the Seven Cities of Cibola. Strangely enough, the Spaniards had brought this myth with them from Europe. According to one account, a Spanish bishop in the 8th century sailed westward from Lisbon, eventually reaching a land where he founded seven flourishing cities.

When the Spaniards arrived in the New World already convinced the story was true, they heard fresh tales from the Indians about a similar legend—that of the Seven Caves, from which a number of tribes had supposedly derived their origins. The similarities were too many to be dismissed as mere coincidence, and soon the two myths merged into one.

Word about the Seven Cities spread quickly, passing from mouth to mouth and tavern to tavern. Cibola—or "Cueola" or Cevola," as it appears in some texts became the very symbol of gold, wealth, and power. It was an earthly paradise, a kingdom of unimagined treasures—if only someone could find it!

The man charged with doing just that was Antonio de Mendoza, viceroy of New Spain. On March 7, 1539, he ordered a small group of explorers accompanied by Pima Indian scouts to march north from Culiacán, which today is the capital of the Mexican state of Sinaloa. Leading the expedition was an unlikely pair: a Franciscan priest named Fray Marcos de Niza and a black Moor whom history knows as Estevánico.

Both men would play a significant role in expanding knowledge of the strange new continent, but their exaggerated reports that came later would undermine their contributions.

As they advanced up the coast of Mexico into what is now the southwestern United States, they encountered Indians who were only too happy to point the way to Cibola. These "Children of the Sun," as they called themselves, promised the strange-skinned explorers that if they kept marching northward they were bound to come across the glittering towers of Cibola sooner or later.

Brimming with optimism, the adventurers trudged onward, visions of wealth surely clouding their minds. After some days on the trail they decided to split up—Estevánico would go one way, Marcos another. Whoever should find the city first would notify the other by sending back a cross.

Less that a week later an Indian from the Moor's escort appeared in Marcos's camp carrying a cross. Marcos couldn't believe his eyes; the Seven Cities of Cibola had been located—and it was only a thirty-day journey to the north!

Marcos set off at once, crossing into present-day Arizona and then northeast into what is now New Mexico. From there he ascended the high Colorado Plateau between the Little

Colorado and the Rio Grande rivers. One night while encamped at this point, he received disquieting news—the Moor was dead. According to an Indian scout, Estevánico had reached the gates of Cibola and was there slaughtered by the occupants who had only moments before befriended him.

Shaken, Fray Marcos resolved not to return to New Spain until he had at least seen Cibola, even if he should die in the attempt. With a handful of frightened Indians he pressed on, crossing more unexplored territory and encountering several other groups of "friendly" Indians who happily directed him toward the city of his dreams.

Then, late one afternoon just as the sun was setting behind a distant range of mountains, the priest came upon a breathtaking sight—down below, in a valley sheltered by a low ring of shimmering hills, he saw the outline of a magnificent city, a city of multi-storied houses and tall towers that sparkled in the fading sunlight. He saw palaces and temples and a great many stone buildings, some rising higher than others.

Without any doubt it was Cibola. He had found the city of gold!

After dedicating the discovery to Saint Francis, he claimed possession of the land for Spain, hitched up his skirts, and sped for home.

News of the priest's discovery spread rapidly throughout New Spain. With each telling of the story, its magnificence grew. Cibola was said to be richer than Tenochtitlán, even more spectacular than the fabled cities of Peru and the Yucatán. Marcos had seen it with his own eyes!

Mendoza now had a decision to make. Since Cibola and the region to the north had already been claimed by Spain, his next step was to send out an expedition of conquest. For this duty he appointed his young friend and fellow aristocrat, Francisco Vásquez de Coronado, the dashing twenty-nine-year-old governor of New Galicia, the northwest province of New Spain.

On February 23, 1540, Coronado and his army of three hundred heavily armed soldiers set off to conquer Cibola, "the greatest country in the world." Coronado's quest would take him across hundreds of miles of parched deserts and rugged mountain ridges, but the rewards would be well worth the hardships.

Around campfires at night the men boasted about what they planned to do with the loot. Most were young and freshly arrived from Spain. Many were already aristocrats, but visions of new wealth nearly drove them into a frenzy as they made their way across the blistering badlands in search of the city of their dreams.

Five months later, in July, the army finally reached Cibola. But Coronado was puzzled; surely this couldn't be the fabulous city of gold Fray Marcos had described. There had to be some mistake. Where were the lofty towers? The gleaming houses studded with precious jewels? What about the palaces and many-stepped temples the priest had reported?

The disappointed commander quickly checked his coordinates. Alas, all the signs indicated he was in the right place. Even the Indians who came running out of the village to greet his retinue matched accounts provided by Marcos.

"The truth about Cibola now lay plainly before them," wrote C. W. Ceram in his exhaustive account of the event in *The First American: A Story of North American Archaeology.* "No mighty monarch reigned here; the doors were not studded with either gold or gems; and the Indians ate from the ground and not from golden dishes."

After capturing the city in the name of the crown, there was only one task left for the dejected conquistador to do— break the dismal tidings to his boss, Mendoza.

"It now remains for me," he wrote, "to tell about this city and kingdom and province of which [Fray Marcos] gave your Lordship an account. In brief, I can assure you that in reality he has not told the truth in a single thing that he said, but everything is the reverse of what he said, except the name of the city and the large stone houses. For, although they are not decorated with turquoises, nor made of lime, nor of good bricks, nevertheless they are very good houses...."

As we now know, Cibola was the "land of the Zunis," a sprawling territory located on the upper Zuni River in New

Mexico and consisting of a modest group of pueblos that were undoubtedly the Seven Cities of Cibola. By any measure, their appearance and wealth fell short of legend and Fray Marcos's claims. To their credit, the people who occupied the region were said to be hard-working and honest individuals who "did not drink...nor eat human flesh nor steal," but they were hardly the handsome men and women who bathed in golden streams and drank from silver goblets, as was rumored.

How could the Spaniards have been so deceived? Why had they been so misinformed about the "desert kingdoms" north of Mexico?

Apparently, their own greed for gold had allowed them to distort reality as they wished. They were not alone. It was a madness that gripped every European capital at the time, coming so soon after the discovery of the New World and the splendid treasure troves in South and Central America.

Cibola was actually only one of several legendary cities of gold said to exist in the wilds of the New World. A decade after his ill-fated search for Cibola, Coronado would be duped into believing another treasured kingdom flourished somewhere in the east.

Quivira was more than just another rumor, according to a Spanish-speaking Plains Indian called El Turco (The Turk). In glowing terms, El Turco told Coronado that there was an abundance of gold in his homeland, and a river "which was two leagues (five miles) wide, in which there were fishes as big as horses, and very big canoes, with more than twenty rowers on a side, and that they carried sails, and that their lords sat on the poop under awnings, and on the prow they had a great golden eagle...."

He also said that everyone had their ordinary dishes "made of wrought plate, and the jugs and bowls were of gold."

Eager for the sight of gold, Coronado's force pushed north from Texas into present-day Oklahoma, then across the Canadian River all the way into Kansas. Finally, after covering about five hundred miles, the Spanish force reached El Turco's Quivira. It was on the Kansas River, exactly where the Indian had said it would be.

But instead of gold and giant canoes, the weary conquistadores found only an encampment of poverty-stricken Wichita Indians, cowering in fear before them and living in grass huts.

Coronado had had enough. This time his disappointment flared into rage and he ordered the immediate execution of the crafty Indian called El Turco.

No more would he be tricked into believing fairytales about golden palaces and bejeweled monarchs in the Godforsaken wilderness!

Bitter and frail, his dreams now shattered, the frustrated commander wheeled his army around and marched back home. But history has been kind to Coronado for his failure to find any legendary city of gold. How can something be found if it isn't there in the first place?

Despite the fiasco of his mission and the reprimand he received from Mendoza upon his return, Coronado's achievements were remarkable. Not only did he blaze a trail across the southwestern United States from Mexico to Kansas, he discovered the Grand Canyon and the Colorado River, and he provided competent reports on the habits and customs of the various Indians of the region.

Mount Shasta's "Mystic Village"

FOR YEARS, PEOPLE LIVING in the remote Siskiyou Mountains of northern California had heard rumors of a mysterious race of people who supposedly lived alone high on the rugged slopes of Mount Shasta, the second tallest peak in the United States.

According to local legend, the elusive mountain dwellers were descended from survivors of Lemuria, an ancient civilization that sank beneath the waves of the Pacific Ocean thousands of years ago during a cataclysmic upheaval. Few outsiders had actually ever seen the Lemurians, even though an estimated six hundred to one thousand were believed to reside on the ancient, cloud-wrapped mountain.

Those who believed in the legend—and their numbers were many—claimed the strange race clung to their old ways in spite of modern encroachment on their habitat. Apparently they still practiced bizarre rituals, and only on rare occasions did they venture down from Mount Shasta to mingle with the lowlanders.

It wasn't until 1932, really, that the outside world became aware of the Mount Shasta legend. That was when the *Los Angeles Times* published an article written by Edward Lanser purporting that an unknown group of people "dressed in spotless white robes" and possessing a large supply of gold had been discovered living in the mountain's higher elevations.

Lanser, who claimed to have visited the Lemurians' "mystic village" and observed their culture first-hand, described the place as "a peaceful community...evidently contented to live as their ancient forebears lived before Lemuria was swallowed by the sea."

Part of Lanser's information for the story came from an interview with Professor Edgar Lucien Larken, a scientist and director of the Mt. Lowe Observatory in southern California, who also supposedly spent time among the Lemurians. What the scientist saw, said Lanser, was "a great temple in the heart of the village—a marvelous work of carved marble and onyx, rivaling in beauty and architectural splendor the magnificence of the temples of Yucatán."

The professor was quoted as saying he had found the unusual villagers "all industriously engaged in the manufacture of articles necessary to their consumption." He said they were also "engaged in farming the sunny slopes and glens surrounding the village—with miraculous results, judging from the astounding vegetation."

During the course of his investigation, Lanser learned that northern Californians had known about the existence of the Lemurians for more than fifty years. Businessmen, explorers, ranchers, and government officials in the region, he said, "spoke freely of the community, and all attested to the weird rituals that were performed on the mountainside after sunset, midnight, and sunrise."

The journalist also learned that only four or five explorers had ever penetrated the "invisible protective boundary of this Lemurian settlement," and of those none had returned to tell the tale.

He added: "The really incredible thing is that these staunch descendants of that vanished race have succeeded in secluding themselves in the midst of our teeming state and that they have managed through some marvelous sorcery to keep highways, hot-dog establishments, filling stations, and the other ugly counterparts of our tourist system out of their sacred precincts."

Each night, said Lanser, the settlers celebrated their escape from Lemuria to "Guatama," as they called America, with brilliant bonfires, elaborate rituals, feasting, and wild singing and dancing. It must have been quite a sight—the "tall, barefooted, noble-looking men and women...clad in spotless white robes" careening around ritualistic blazes beneath the clustered clouds and brooding shadows of the surrounding Siskiyou, their voices echoing through the black and virgin forest.

Sometimes—but not often—the Lemurians would wander down the mountain to nearby towns to buy lard, sulphur, salt, and other staples. Such goods were often paid for in gold nuggets, prompting much speculation and not a few raised eyebrows among the lowland merchants with whom they traded.

With the passage of time, however, memories of the "mystic village" have all but disappeared. Few folks living in the region now have ever even heard of the legend, let alone claim to having witnessed their rituals or heard their ancient song floating on the still night air.

As with the golden cities of Cibola and El Dorado, as with Atlantis and even ancient Lemuria itself, there are those who still believe passionately in the legend of Mount Shasta, many of them unaware or forgetful of the fact that the story itself probably had its origins in the publication in 1894 of an occultistic novel called *A Dweller on Two Planets*.

In the book, written by Frederick Spencer Oliver, the narrator is wandering among the solitary haunts of Mount Shasta when he encounters a Chinese mystic named Quong. As it turns out, Quong is no ordinary coolie—he's one of the masters of a group of mysterious magi who have supernatural powers and are able to communicate freely with animals. With the other magi, Quong resides on a misty back slope of Mount Shasta where the wisdom of the ages is a closely guarded secret.

These supermen, however, decide to induct the narrator into their brotherhood, and then bestow upon him some of their spiritual powers, including the ability to body-travel to other planets.

For more than three decades, nobody paid much attention to Oliver's rambling, tedious novel, which incidentally belonged more to the realm of pseudo-science than fantasy fiction. But with the publication of *Lemuria, the Lost Continent of the Pacific* in 1931 by Cerve, a new age of American mysticism was dawning. In his book—drawn heavily from Oliver's strange tale and containing elements of theosophy, Christian Science, Ballardism, and Rosicrucianism—Cerve drops dark hints of mysterious inscriptions at nearby Klamath Falls, unaccountable lights at night, and other mysteries around Mount Shasta.

Instead of a mystical kingdom ruled by Chinese magi, however, Cerve reveals a shadowy domain occupied by long-haired beings of angelic descent who speak with English accents and pilot "boat-shaped" aircraft high above the rainy peaks of the ancient Siskiyou.

Today the "mystic village" and its white-robed inhabitants are, of course, long gone. Where roaring bonfires once blazed and the weird tunes of an ancient race once echoed softly, there is now the hubbub of campers and hikers and forest rangers roaming freely among the misty forests of Mount Shasta.

The Moving Stones of Death Valley

AT THE EASTERN EDGE OF southern California is a vast, windswept desert, one of the loneliest and least habitable regions on earth. At three hundred feet below sea level, Death Valley National Monument is also the lowest, driest, hottest place in the United States.

For centuries, the Indians regarded this desolate domain as a spirit-filled netherworld, a place to be avoided at all costs. Conquistadores and then generations of reckless pioneers entering the forbidden valley soon learned—the hard way—why the Indians stayed away. Today their bleached and brittle bones still litter the parched sand.

Except for scientists and an occasional group of adventurous tourists, few people visit Death Valley. Those who do are often astounded by what many consider one of the world's most puzzling natural phenomena—the "moving stones."

Ranging in size from pebbles to boulders, the stones appear to move across the arid landscape, leaving behind long, swirling trails to mark their passing. Some tracks zig-zag in irregular patterns, others circle gracefully across the desert floor, while a few stream directly behind the stones in straight lines for hundreds of feet.

The strange thing about the stones is that nobody has ever actually seen them move. It's as if some unseen force guides the rocks along their slow, ghostly journey—but only when there are no human witnesses around.

At Racetrack Playa, for example, a dried-up lake on the edge of the valley, the clay and sand floor is streaked with tracks made by the creeping rocks. Geologists studying the mystery in 1968 reported that one large rock moved more than 860 feet in several movements, while a nine-ounce pebble tumbled 690 feet in the single biggest move.

What causes the stones to move? Nobody really knows, but over the years numerous theories have emerged to account for the puzzle. Some claim that a strange force is behind the oddity—a magnetic field, perhaps, or mysterious vibrations, or some other unknown physical or even mystical power. A few believe the stones are swept along by rushing floods, while others see a connection with reported UFO activity in the area.

Until a few years ago, the whole thing was treated pretty much as a joke, even among scientists. It was widely believed for a while that people living on the outer fringes of the desert would drive into the valley at night and manually move the stones before busloads of tourists arrived the next morning to gawk and wonder.

Those possibilities seem to evaporate when certain factors are taken into account, such as the numbers of rocks moved and the enormous size of some of the boulders. Who would be foolish or driven enough to enter the snake-infested desert at night just to move hundreds, and sometimes thousands, of pebbles and boulders? What would have been the incentive? Tourism? That's highly unlikely, since the few bands of adventurers who visit the stones each year aren't enough to make such a hoax profitable.

Dr. Robert P. Sharp, a professor of geology at the California Institute of Technology, thinks he knows the answer. After a seven-year study of the stones—during which he tagged dozens of stones and even gave them pet names such as Mary Ann, Milly, Jane, Margie, and Nancy—Sharp came to the conclusion that movement is caused by the combined forces of wind and water.

Sharp theorizes that moisture on the hard, clay-packed surface of the lake floor creates conditions slick enough for the stones to slide over during a strong wind. Powerful breezes channeled down from the nearby Grapevine Mountains are often sufficient, says the professor, to send the stones skidding across the Playa surface at a pace described as "something more than a slow creep."

In a report released after completion of his study, Sharp said conditions have to be "just right" in order for the peculiar movements to occur.

"Wetting of the Playa surface is required to the extent that a thin, slimy, water-saturated mud layer overlies a still firm base," he wrote. "This condition is attained within an hour or two after water gathers on the surface. Stained areas forward of some moved stones suggest that only a thin film of water lay on the Playa surface at the time these stones moved."

Since no one has ever seen the rocks move, there are those who doubt the veracity of Sharp's conclusion. A few scientists theorize that the stones are rocked along by periodic ice storms.

And there are those who cling to the notion that aliens from outer space somehow direct the movement of the stones for purposes still unclear. Not long ago, a report was circulated among UFO watchers that electro-magnetic vibrations emitted by alien spacecraft operating in the area caused the stones to glide silently and mysteriously across the barren desert floor.

Whatever moves them, Death Valley's strange traveling stones continue to intrigue visitors and scientists alike. And, as with the pyramids of Egypt and the stone heads of Easter Island, it is doubtful the enigmatic stones of Death Valley will ever reveal their true secret.

The Return of a Lost Village

LONG BEFORE THE COMING of the white man, a solitary tribe of Indians known as the Makan lived along the rugged shores of the Pacific Ocean in the northwestern corner of what is now called Washington.

Not much is known about these ancient tribesmen except that they were excellent craftsmen and even better fishermen. They were also great storytellers, a gift passed down to the present generation of Makah, who continue to occupy the same region as their mysterious ancestors.

Of all the great stories of the Makah, however, none is more intriguing than that of "the day the mountain moved." For centuries, tribal elders have told the story of how, one day many centuries ago, a mountain of mud descended upon their tiny village of Ozette, burying everything and everybody in its path.

Some of the ancients escaped. Many did not. For centuries, their bones lay buried beneath tons of soft soil and rocks along the heavily wooded coastline.

Since there were no written records of the disaster, the story was kept alive by voices. Around campfires and crackling hearths, the story was told and retold. By the 20th century, the catastrophic event at Ozette had become a legend firmly ingrained in the mythology of the Northwest Indians.

It seemed an unlikely story, of course, but one man thought otherwise. He was Richard Daugherty, professor of anthropology at Washington State University. For years Daugherty had suspected the Ozette legend was true. But how could he prove it? Like Heinrich Schliemann and Sir Arthur Evans before him, all he had to go on was a hunch—and the time-honored legends swirling around the truth.

Then one chilly February morning in 1970, the truth was unveiled for Daugherty. A winter storm had swept in the night before, surging up the broad beach and battering the banks beyond. All night long the savage winds ripped at the shores, while torrential rainfall pummeled from above.

By dawn the storm had passed—but not before part of the bank had given way in an avalanche of mud. Later that morning, a hiker out surveying the damage happened to stumble across an unusual-looking object protruding from the mud. At first he thought it was a piece of driftwood, then he realized its angles were much too clean and definite to be anything but man-made.

Fortunately for Daugherty, the hiker reported his find to the authorities. As soon as news reached him that the storm had uncovered artifacts where ancient Ozette once stood, the archaeologist raced to the scene, shovel in hand. The first thing he examined was the object found by the hiker. Clearly, Daugherty reasoned, it was a paddle—a well-preserved old paddle unlike anything seen around these parts since ancient times.

As he worked in the cold mud, Daugherty couldn't help imagining the unfortunate Indian to whom the paddle had belonged, an Indian buried beneath a mountain of mud hundreds of years ago. If there was a paddle, then surely there must be a canoe. If there was a canoe, there might be a house, and if he could find a house, then surely he would find human remains—all links to the mysterious lost village of Ozette.

Was he on the verge of uncovering the long-lost land of the Makah? Was this where the Indians had suffered their legendary disaster?

Surely similar thoughts came to Howard Carter as he stood before the inner chamber of Tutankhamen's tomb, and to Austen Henry Layard as he prepared to lay bare the charred ruins of mighty Nineveh. Like the giants of archaeology before him, Daugherty gave his imagination free rein as he contemplated the scientific and historical implications of the secrets perhaps buried beneath his feet.

The professor's dream merged into reality later that day when the site yielded more tangible proof of a much earlier occupation. Fishhooks, a harpoon shaft, part of a carved wooden box, and a woven-straw hat were among the first treasures brought forth from the mud near where the paddle had been found.

Radiocarbon dating confirmed what Daugherty already suspected—the artifacts were old, very old, dating from a period before Columbus's arrival in the New World. They had survived intact for centuries because the heavy blanket of mud blocked out air and kept them from decay.

While boxes of carefully marked artifacts were being filled and carted away for study, more evidence of antiquity was beginning to surface—first a timber wall, then a complete house filled with cooking utensils, sleeping platforms, and assorted personal belongings. Also inside the sixty-five-foot-long house were the remains of several human beings who apparently had been entombed when the wall of mud came crashing down more than five centuries ago.

Among the many items unearthed within the great dwelling were fishnets, wooden bowls, and a handsome cedar carving of a whale's fin, inlaid with more than seven hundred sea-otter teeth. There were toys strewn about, including wooden bats shaped like ping-pong paddles, shuttlecocks made of thimbleberry stem, and even a tiny bow-and-arrow set.

Excavation was tedious. Tons of wet earth had to be removed bucket by bucket. Carefully directed streams of water from hoses delicately washed clean the fragile remains of a vanished civilization.

In the end, once the mud of centuries had been cleared away and the pieces reassembled, the ancient village of Ozette gleamed fresh and new in the sunlight.

In a sense, it was a happy ending to the tragedy that brought death and destruction to a seaside village more than five hundred years ago. Daugherty called the discovery "truly a national treasure…[the] most significant and unique find in northwest coast archaeology."

For the modern Indians, whose forefathers had been swallowed by a mountain of mud so long ago, the excavation—which is still ongoing—means more. As one member of the tribe put it: "We look in a special way at what is coming from the mud at Ozette, for this is our heritage."

Unnatural Worlds

Firestarters and Firewalkers

LITTLE WILLIE BROUGH WAS only twelve years old when his parents accused him of being possessed by the devil and threw him out of their San Francisco house.

Willie knew he had it coming. Still, he wondered why his mom and dad didn't understand his problem. It was a "special" problem that made him an outcast at his school. Even the kids at church didn't like to play with him anymore; if they weren't making jokes about him behind his back, they were running away like scared jackrabbits.

But his own parents? You'd think they'd care enough about their own son at least to listen to his side of the story.

Willie's problem wasn't fighting or staying out late or teasing girls. On the contrary, he was always home on time for supper, never quarreled about getting up for school, and went about his chores cheerfully.

He was a good boy, a model son in every way but one.

Everywhere Willie went, things seemed to catch fire. At school, it might be a desk or a textbook; at church, it was usually the pew; at home, it was curtains, bedcovers, clothing, and tablecloths. Once, when he was standing next to his mother, her dress caught fire.

It had been that way ever since he could remember. There was never any explanation, either. Willie would simply walk into a room, or sit on a chair, or lie on a bed, and flames would start shooting from some nearby object—furniture, clothing, floors, ceilings, books. He couldn't control it, no matter how hard he tried.

Deep down, Willie couldn't blame his parents for ordering him out of their house. It was the only thing they could do. If he had a clue about what was causing the strange fires, maybe he could do something. But he didn't have a clue. They just seemed to break out wherever he went and whatever he did. It worried him, of course, but he was powerless to do anything about it.

Then, in 1886, his parents finally decided they'd had enough. The boy's curious power scared them real bad. That was understandable: all he had to do was look at an object, and it would burst into flames.

Only the devil could cause such a thing, they reasoned, so the best thing was simply to get rid of the boy, their only son. Satan would have to go do his business in some other household. They were tired of having their furniture and clothes destroyed by his evil hand.

So out into the street Willie went one morning, suitcase in hand, the smell of singed furniture fresh in his nostrils. He had no idea where to go or what to do. He just wandered through the streets for a few days, grabbing handouts where he could, trying to stay out of trouble.

Then one day a local farmer heard about the homeless boy. His heart was touched. He felt sorry for him and decided to take him in. It didn't take the farmer long to realize he'd made a big mistake.

The first day Willie was in his new home, fires broke out—first in the kitchen, then in an upstairs bedroom. The farmer and his wife calmly dismissed those incidents and got the boy ready for school the next morning. It was a new school to Willie, of course, with a new teacher and new classmates.

Weird things started up the moment he walked into the classroom. The teacher's desk suddenly caught fire—then a student's desk. Later, when things had quieted down after the first two fires, a pair of curtains suddenly burst into flames.

Altogether, seven fires disrupted the classroom that first day—two on the wall, another in the teacher's wardrobe, and one, strangest of all, in the center of the classroom ceiling. The teacher and students put two and two together and concluded that Willie was somehow behind the rash of blazes.

What kind of freak was this new kid, anyway?

Willie's first day at the new school was his last. The trustees, convinced that the new boy was responsible for the series of fires, promptly expelled him. It seemed the only logical thing to do given his past record. No school board could tolerate a pyromaniac in the halls and classrooms.

Nobody knows what became of little Willie Brough, but in recent years researchers have put together enough information to realize that the boy did, indeed, have a special kind of uncontrollable problem. And he was not alone. Apparently hundreds of unsuspecting people over the years have been possessed with a unique power—the power simply to look at objects and make them catch fire.

These people are known as "firestarters." Although no one knows why or how, the presence of firestarters alone is seemingly sufficient to spark a conflagration.

For example, in 1895 an estimated twenty-five fires broke out in the Brooklyn home of Adam Colwell—all in one day! Even police called in to investigate watched furniture burst into flames without apparent cause. One fireman who responded to the call saw wallpaper ignite and begin to burn.

In the Colwell case, the finger of suspicion soon pointed to the family's adopted daughter, Rhoda, a pretty young teenager who wept openly when accused of being responsible for the fires. Her guilt seemed sealed, however, when a former employer of Rhoda's came forward and claimed that numerous fires had started in his Flushing, New York, residence a few months earlier when the girl had worked for him as a maid.

During a gruelling police interrogation, Rhoda broke down in tears and "confessed" that she had, in fact, caused the fires. She hadn't the faintest notion how, but she was sure they were her fault, because everywhere she had ever gone, smoke and fire always followed.

Mysterious outbreaks of fires have plagued certain people down through the ages. Firestarters were apparently around in ancient Greece, as they were in Medieval Europe. The Bible describes several suspicious cases, while in Africa and the Far East, many more have been reported.

Equally mysterious are those people who appear to have been totally immune to fire. The historical record contains numerous accounts of those who can swallow flames, press hot pokers to their faces, and calmly stroll through beds of burning coals without feeling the slightest discomfort.

In 1927, for example, a New York doctor on a hunting trip in the Tennessee mountains met a shy backwoods boy who could handle a pair of glowing firebrands without suffering any harm.

More than four decades earlier, a muscular young blacksmith from Easton, Maryland, named Nathan Coker was in the habit of astonishing onlookers—including the mayor of New York City—with his unusual ability to walk across white-hot coals from his furnace. *The New York Herald* reported that after a shovel had been heated to a white glow, the aptly named Coker pulled off his boots, placed the shovel against the soles of his feet, and kept it there until it cooled to black.

The newspaper and dozens of other witnesses also testified that the blacksmith swilled molten lead shot around in his mouth until it solidified, held glowing coals in his hands, and with the same bare hands extracted a red-hot iron from the fire.

"It don't burn," he told the startled spectators. "Since I was a boy, I've never been afraid to handle fire."

In 1882, several newspapers in the northeast carried stories about a Paw Paw, Michigan, prankster who could allegedly create fire by holding a handkerchief to his mouth and breathing on it. To demonstrate the veracity of his act, the man would strip, wash out his mouth, then borrow another handkerchief from the audience and start a fire all over again simply by breathing on it.

How is it that some people are totally oblivious to the harmful effects of flame and smoke while others scorch and gag whenever they get within a few feet of a blaze?

One psychic investigator suggested that the ability to fire-walk or fire-start illustrates a different dimension of reality in which fire does not burn in the familiar way. This might also explain how some people suddenly burst into flames them-selves—a rare but documented phenomenon known as "spontaneous human combustion," or SHC.

But that's another story.

Bi-location: Worlds Without Walls

ED MORRELL COULDN'T take it any more.

For the past four years, they had done everything they could to break his spirit. They had beaten him, tortured him, humiliated him beyond belief. Every bone in his body ached. His flesh quivered with pain from the tracks of pin and needle marks and cigarette burns.

When they finally strapped him in a water-soaked straightjacket and threw him into a dark pit, the young Arizona State Prison inmate knew he was a goner unless he could figure out a way to escape.

But how?

The answer came a few nights later.

Writhing in pain on his cell floor, scarcely able to breath because of a brutal beating inflicted on him earlier by a couple of sadistic guards, young Morrell suddenly felt the pain slipping away like air leaking from a tube. His first thought was that he was dying. He rolled over on his back, gasping, wheezing, clinging to life.

As if by magic, the intolerable pain went away. In its place was a rush of tremendous pleasure—a light, floating sensation that made his head swim with delight.

What was going on?

Never in his life had Morrell felt so wonderfully, marvelously *free!*

Sometime later—it couldn't have been more than a few seconds—Morrell felt himself slowly rising toward the ceiling.

His body hadn't moved, because he could see it, still curled up on the cell floor below.

Morrell's miracle was only beginning.

Before he knew it, he felt his "second body" passing through the cell walls, gliding across the prison yard, then drifting cloudlike beyond the main walls. Although there were dozens of guards below, no effort was made to stop him. It was as if he were invisible, an unseen spirit floating through the clouds.

Then Morrell discovered something else—he could "wish" himself anywhere he wanted to go, just by concentrating hard and visualizing his destination. All night long, he visited distant cities and faraway places, drifting low, a shimmering, unseen light hovering between the clouds.

The next morning, he awoke fresh and in good spirits. The first thing he thought about was his incredible voyage. Surely he had been dreaming; nothing so fantastic could happen to a human being unless—the thought chilled him to the bone—he was dead.

But here he was, eating breakfast, listening to the surly guards clomp around outside his cell, very much alive. He felt afraid and confused. What had really happened? Had he died, then somehow come back to life? Or was it something else?

That night, reeling from another brutal beating at the hands of the guards, Morrell felt himself slipping back into the same twilight state of euphoria he had experienced earlier. Next thing he knew, he was floating over the prison and away into the clouds, just like before. Some time later he awoke in his cell, once again feeling refreshed.

Though he didn't understand what was happening to him, Morrell soon decided to take advantage of the situation. Why not? Apparently he could "escape" prison whenever he wanted to. The only catch, of course, was that he always had to return because his physical body was still behind bars. In time, Morrell learned how to deal with his uncanny ability, and the remainder of his time in prison became more tolerable.

Like all people who have experienced "out-of-body" experiences, Morrell was convinced he was not dreaming or hallucinating. On a number of trips, he witnessed events which he was later able to confirm really happened. Also he saw people who were strangers to him at the time but, whom he later met. One of these strangers was his future wife.

Ironically, as soon as he was released from prison four years later, Morrell lost his ability to leave his body at will. In his book *The Twenty-Fifth Man*, Morrell described in detail some of his more unusual adventures. He theorized that the pain and misery of prison had brought on his unearthly trips.

Each year dozens of people around the world report similar out-of-body experiences. Few, however, say they travel as often or as far as Morrell. Such experiences frequently occur on operating tables in hospitals or following accidents, and their descriptions usually match those provided by Morrell.

People living in the 20th century aren't the first to experience out-of-body travel. History is replete with stories of individuals crossing the threshold, only to return and tell about their adventures. As part of their religious ceremonies, some American Indian tribes deliberately practiced mortification of the physical body for the purpose of traveling through the spirit world, seeking information, or guiding the dead into the afterworld.

In the early 17th century, the Catholic Church launched a full investigation into a story about a Spanish nun who claimed to be able to transport herself spiritually and bodily to the New World. The presence of Sister María Agreda has been recorded by American Indians, Mexicans, and Spanish conquistadores serving in the southwestern United States.

One of the most celebrated cases of bi-location, as the condition is called in scientific circles, involved a noted New York medium, Mrs. Eileen Garrett. While under the observation of scientists, Mrs. Garrett was able to project herself at will to any location—all the way to Reykjavik, Iceland, on one occasion, where she was able to reveal what a participating scientist there was wearing, eating, and reading. At one point, she reportedly read aloud over the doctor's shoulder a passage from the book he was reading

Only in recent years has the out-of-body projection phenomenon been systematically studied by psychologists, parapsychologists, and physicists. At the Stanford Research Institute in California, two physicists tested the ability of certain people to project their consciousness to a distant location and give a correct report of what they could see there.

The experiments conducted by Doctors Harold Puthoff and Russell Targ led them to the conclusion that "remote perceptual abilities" can be exercised, after a period of training, by people who would not have suspected themselves of possessing any paranormal abilities.

Perhaps the most famous person to go on record as having experienced "astral projection" was Ernest Hemingway. It happened during World War I, he wrote, seconds after a mortar shell exploded near him.

"I felt my soul or something coming right out of my body, like you'd pull a silk handkerchief out of a pocket by one corner. It flew around and then came back and went in again, and I wasn't dead anymore."

According to those who have tried it, out-of-body experiences can be delightful, though frightful—reminders, they claim, that some part of the human body survives death.

Raining Steaks and Snakes

ON FRIDAY, MARCH 3, 1876, Mr. and Mrs. Allen Crouch had just sat down at the supper table when they were startled by an unusual slapping sound from the tin roof of their rural home in Bath County, Kentucky.

It sounded like rain, so the middle-aged couple sprang to check the windows. Not a drop of rain had fallen, nor was there a cloud in sight.

For several long seconds, they stood peering out the windows into the dry, dusty twilight, wondering what was making the sound. Then something strange happened. A piece of meat, measuring about four inches square and resembling fresh beef, flopped through the open window.

"Saints alive," Mrs. Crouch gasped, making the sign of the cross as she stepped back from the huge chunk of "pleasant-tasting" meat.

Soon another piece of meat of equal size fell through the window. Then another and another. Within seconds, the floor of the tiny kitchen was covered with chunks of meat of various sizes and states of freshness. The Crouches had to move back from the window to keep from being splattered by the torrent of meat showering through the window.

A few seconds later, the "deluge" stopped almost as suddenly as it had begun. Slowly Allen Crouch poked his head out the window. Satisfied that nothing more was falling, he moved toward the door.

Crouch went outside and couldn't believe his eyes. Everywhere he looked, he saw bloody pieces of meat. The yard was covered; so was the porch. He figured at least a ton of the stuff had fallen onto his house and yard.

But what was it?

Next morning, several neighbors came over to examine the mysterious skyfall for themselves. So did a couple of reporters who even volunteered to taste the meat. In their story, they identified the strange stuff as "either mutton or venison."

Where had it come from? Nobody—not even scientists who came to investigate—had a clue. Some neighbors thought it was a gift from God. Others weren't so sure; maybe the devil had sent it.

Whatever the source, the Bath County skyfall was one of the biggest news stories in Kentucky that year. But less than a year later, on a hot Sunday afternoon in 1877, a skyfall in Memphis, Tennessee, would overshadow the Kentucky meat shower.

It had come out of nowhere, catching the city off guard. In the near-frenzy that followed it is remarkable that no one was hurt or killed as they scattered for shelter. As strollers and churchgoers huddled inside doorways and beneath over-hangs, thousands of living snakes—some of them poisonous—fell from the skies, covering rooftops, yards, gardens, streets, and sidewalks.

Pedestrians watched in horror as the wriggling masses of serpents slithered away in all directions. Some stayed where they landed, coiled and hissing. One bewildered rider jumped off his horse when a large reptile draped itself around the animal's neck.

When the aerial invasion was over and city officials had safely rounded up and destroyed the snakes, citizens held special church services and prayer meetings. Scientists rushed to the scene from as far away as New York and Boston.

The mysterious rain of snakes was officially attributed to a freak storm that had sprung up over a nearby swamp, sweeping up the snakes and depositing them over the city. No one bothered to explain why only snakes had been snatched by the storm and not rabbits, squirrels, turtles, and other small creatures.

Similar skyfalls in other parts of the United States have intrigued and terrified generations of Americans. One of the most incredible occurred in Charleston, South Carolina, in 1883, when a fully grown alligator dropped from the sky at the corner of Wentworth and Anson Streets!

Eight years later in 1901, catfish, perch, "and a few that looked like trout" showered Kershaw County in Utah. In June, 1957, thousands of fish, worms, and snakes covered Magnolia Terminal in Thomasville, Alabama. A similar skyfall occurred in 1841, when fish and a ten-inch squid landed on Boston.

Among the objects to fall from clear blue skies have been hot bricks, iced ducks, gopher turtles encased in ice, lizards, and frogs. Hailstones the size of softballs are frequently reported, as are "hot" rocks and pebbles.

What are we to make of these strange gifts from the sky? Over the years, numerous theories have come forth, many of them more bizarre than the actual events themselves. Explanations have ranged from the scientific to the supernatural, from black holes and extra-dimensional connections to poltergeists and otherworldly mischief-makers.

The most likely causes are freak windstorms that sweep in across a forest, swamp, or ocean gathering up light creatures and objects and depositing them over some distant location. Scientists have observed such actions in nature, but so far no scientists have been able to explain how tons of fresh mutton and venison were scooped up and dropped onto the property of the Allen Crouch farm in Kentucky on hot, dry night more than a century ago.

The Man Who Cheated Death

ON THE NIGHT OF OCTOBER 31, 1926, a short, muscular, middle-aged man complaining of stomach cramps admitted himself to Grace Hospital in Detroit for observation. His condition was quickly diagnosed as acute appendicitis, and doctors went to work immediately to remove the ruptured organ.

In spite of a gallant effort, the doctor's failed. Toxins from the man's damaged appendix had seeped into his bloodstream. A few hours later, the patient lapsed into a deep coma, and then died just as the sun was rising over the dark waters of lake St. Clair.

The man's body was shipped to New York, where thousands of mourners filed past his open casket inside the huge ballroom of the Elks Lodge on West 43rd Street. Entertainers and politicians from all over the world attended the funeral, as did famous artists, scientists, and writers, including close friend, Sir Arthur Conan Doyle.

After a final farewell by an attending rabbi, the gleaming bronze coffin was sealed and taken away. Many of those present half expected to see the coffin lid snap open any second and the familiar form within spring triumphantly out to a standing ovation.

The man inside the silk-lined coffin was Harry Houdini himself, modern history's supreme illusionist, escapologist, and grand magician. For thirty-five years, Houdini had been the living symbol of man's ancient desire to conjure up mysterious forces that defied nature—defied even death itself.

This time the master would disappoint the hopeful crowd. This time there would be no flourish of trumpets or drum roll or cloud of smoke. Harry Houdini, born Ehrich Weiss, fifth child of a Hungarian rabbi, the man who had cheated death hundreds of times in the past with his daring feats and dazzling illusions, was dead.

In death, Houdini would remain as controversial as in life. Today, more than six decades after his passing, legions of hopeful followers insist it's only a matter of time before the master returns—whether in flesh or spirit. In 1990, magic lovers led by the illusionist Kreskin gathered in Marshall, Michigan, to attempt to communicate with the legendary magician through mental telepathy and a series of séances.

The effort failed, but Kreskin remains convinced that contact with the spirit world is possible. He has offered one million dollars to anyone who can pass a test designed to provide evidence of psychic phenomena.

Psychic manifestations, Ouija boards, and other paranormal activities were familiar to Houdini, a spiritualist who spent a small fortune trying to establish contact with his beloved dead mother. When everything failed, he grew deeply bitter toward psychic mediums and launched a strenuous campaign to expose trick séances. He would eventually turn against his friend Sir Arthur Conan Doyle because of the writer's uncompromising views on spiritualism.

Harry Houdini, appropriately, was as strange and, in many ways, as baffling as the magic he created. One moment moody and withdrawn—often brooding in his consuming devotion to his mother—and the next, charming and polite, bristling with energy and an uncompromising obsession to become the best showman in the business.

His craving for success, a force which had propelled him out of abject poverty into tremendous wealth, began humbly enough when he went to work as a child to help support his impoverished immigrant parents. At the age of seventeen, young Ehrich bought a secondhand book that was to transform his life. It was the memoirs of Jean Eugene Robert-

Houdin, a dazzling French illusionist and magician who could produce cannonballs from an empty hat.

Deeply impressed, the boy vowed to become a magician, too. Later, struggling on the vaudeville circuit, he changed his name to Harry Houdini in honor of and respect for his famous French inspiration. Like Houdin, Houdini was intrigued by escapology—the art of escaping from tightly bound ropes or other forms of bondage, which had been a traditional act in traveling shows and circuses down through the centuries.

Young Houdini studied his craft religiously, finally mastering the secrets of rope escapes. He also taught himself how to swallow handfuls of needles; shed strait jackets, manacles, and chains; and get free from steel safes and a variety of other locked and secured spaces. One of his regular acts was to make a ten-thousand-pound elephant disappear from a wooden cage.

In short, there was no form of bondage from which the popular, persuasive-tongued illusionist could not escape. In Europe, where his career actually began, as well as in Asia, America, and South America, Houdini's glittering displays of magic, escape, and illusion were being billed as "The Greatest Novelty Mystery Act in the World!" From the squalor of a Manhattan immigrant ghetto, Harry Houdini had come to be one of the most famous and highly paid entertainers in the world, commanding upwards of four thousand dollars per show.

Nothing, it seemed, could prevent the tousle-haired magician from escaping the impossible. Chained, tied, and taped inside steel boxes lowered into the sea, he repeatedly stumped onlookers by escaping and making his way to the surface—sometimes in seconds! He once offered a three thousand dollar prize to anyone who could find a concealed key, spring, or lock pick; no challengers ever came forward.

One of his most popular performances was to hang suspended from tall buildings, bound and locked into strait-jackets or sacks. While crowds of hushed spectators watched from below, the master would slip free and gracefully descend a supporting rope or cable. On another occasion, he escaped from a sealed water drum filled with beer—"and me a teetotaler," he quipped to the audience.

The strenuous demands of his performance work had developed for Houdini a hard, well-muscled body, which he boasted could withstand blows from any fist. He often had takers and would usually laugh at their efforts to make him wince.

During one stop in Montreal, a student from McGill University stepped forward and delivered four pile-driving blows to Houdini's middle. The master cheerfully accepted the blows but later, during the second half of the show, felt a sudden stabbing pain in his stomach. The show went on, but that night he awoke his wife, Bess, complaining of what he thought was a cramp.

Two days later on the way to another show in Detroit, hot needles of pain flashed through Houdini's stomach and his temperature soared. Upon arrival, a doctor informed the magician he was suffering from acute appendicitis. The place for Harry, he said, was home in bed, not on stage.

Refusing the doctor's advice, Houdini went on with the show as usual. It was a full and exhausting act, and all the while, he worked in extreme agony. After the final curtain, he was taken back to his hotel. About three a.m., he was rushed to Detroit's Grace Hospital.

By then it was too late. The toxins from his ruptured appendix had already infected his system. Two hours later, he died in Bess's arms.

Harry Houdini, the greatest magician who ever lived, had made his last escape.

Secrets from Beyond

Ghostly Rappings from Beyond

ONE STORMY NIGHT IN THE spring of 1848, a family of five sat huddled around the hearth inside their lonely log cabin near Hydesville, New York.

For more than half an hour, they had been listening spellbound to a strange noise echoing through the house, a noise that sounded like unseen hands clapping to an unheard beat.

At first John Fox thought a window or hinge must be loose, banging around in the fierce wind. When a room-to-room search failed to reveal any cause for the noise, he gathered his wife and children near him in the living room to await the dawn and, he hoped, the end of the demonic noise.

Sometime during the night, the Fox family discovered they could communicate with the unseen power by making knocking noises themselves.

It was the youngest daughter, Kate, age seven, who conducted the first test. Clapping her hands, she challenged whatever it was making the sound to respond—which it did immediately. "Do as I do," she said. The raps repeated the number of claps.

Then the second daughter, Margaret, age ten, joined in. "No, do as I do!" she shouted. "Count one, two, three, four." Four raps came in response, frightening the young girl so much she refused to play the game anymore.

It soon occurred to Mr. Fox that the noises were being produced by an unseen intelligence. Various members of the family established a dialogue by asking questions and getting either one rap for "yes" or two raps for "no." In this way, they learned that the rapping was made by a peddler who had been murdered and buried beneath the house years ago.

The ghostly sounds continued for the next several months, sometimes waking the Fox family in the middle of the night. Although after the first few nights they never really felt threatened, they decided the only way to find peace again was to move—which they did. But, amazingly, everywhere they went, the sounds soon followed.

Then one night a few years later, the third and oldest Fox sister received a bizarre message from beyond. By reciting the alphabet and asking the noises to respond at the correct letter, Leah Fox decoded the following words:

"Dear friends, you must proclaim this truth to the world. This is the dawning of a new era; you must not try to conceal it any longer. When you do your duty, God will protect you and good spirits will watch over you."

From that moment on, the Fox sisters knew they had been charged with a special purpose in life. They would be ridiculed, and perhaps persecuted by an uncaring materialistic world, but their purpose was unmistakably clear—to establish and maintain contact with the spirits of people who had passed on beyond the Great Plane.

A few weeks later, they began holding special sessions to enable departed spirits to communicate with grieving relatives and friends left behind. As a result, what might have been no more than another fascinating ghost story became instead the founding of a religious movement which quickly spread around the globe.

For the next half century, until their own deaths in the late 1800s, the Fox Sisters—Leah, Kate, and Margaret—enjoyed celebrity as the leading spiritualists of their time. Although other mediums and psychics claimed to be successful in communicating with the dead, it was the presence of one or all of the Fox sisters that usually assured success.

In time, the three girls founded the Society for the Diffusion of Spiritual Knowledge, which sponsored free public sittings. Into their heavily-draped parlors or "reading rooms" sauntered some of the richest and most powerful civic, cultural, political, and business leaders of the day—including Horace Greeley, the editor of the prestigious *New York Tribune*—to listen, to talk, to feel veiled and shrouded presences from beyond.

On certain occasions when the Fox sisters felt strong enough, they were able to bring forth the physical forms and voices of the dead. These manifestations were sometimes represented by long glowing streams of protoplasm protruding from the medium's mouth, eyes, nose, and ears.

At other times, they were able to make tables, chairs, and even people levitate. Their astonishing gifts did not go unreported.

After his first visit to the Fox sisters, Horace Greeley wrote, "Whatever may be the origin or cause of the 'rapping,' the ladies in whose presence they occur do not make them. We tested this thoroughly and to our entire satisfaction."

Other famous journalists, scientists, clergymen, and experts in paranormal phenomena flocked to the Fox sisters' parlors to investigate the so-called spirit manifestations. In 1861, rich New York banker Charles F. Livermore hired Kate to act as his private medium—which she did for five years, conducting nearly four hundred seances during which Livermore tried to contact his dead wife, Estelle. It was during the forty-third session that Livermore is said to have recognized her ghostly form and heard her speak a few words.

The career of the Fox sisters soon fell under a dark cloud. In April of 1851, Margaret Fox allegedly told a relative that her work was all a hoax. The confession, however, did little to stem the popularity of this fast-growing quasi-religious movement that continued to gain thousands of supporters around the world.

Then, on May 27, 1888, the *New York Herald* reported that Margaret had once again confessed to fraud. According to the story, she told how she and her sisters had been able to simulate ghostly rappings from beyond by snapping the joints of their toes and ankles.

Still, a sensation-starved public refused to accept Margaret's astonishing second confession—even when Kate joined her sister two months later in revealing how they had duped the public. For reasons that remain mysterious, both sisters withdrew their confessions a year later, saying they had been forced to make them because of pressing financial problems.

The public didn't know what to believe any more. Mediums or frauds? Mystics or fakes? Just what were these Fox sisters, and what did they possibly hope to gain from changing their stories so many times?

While the debate raged on in the newspapers and in drawing rooms, there were plenty of other talented mediums more than willing to step in and take over for the famous Fox sisters—mediums who profited handsomely from a growing fascination for spiritualism in America.

By 1893, the last of the Fox sisters had died, taking to her grave the secrets of their trade. Even in death, however, the trio continues to be held in the highest esteem as Spiritualism's (perhaps) immortal founders.

Phantom Windows into the Past

MRS. COLEEN BATERBAUGH was in a happy mood on the morning of October 3, 1963, as she strolled briskly across the leaf-strewn campus of Nebraska Wesleyan University in Lincoln. She had every reason to be upbeat—her boss, Dean Sam Dahl, had just given her a raise, and on top of that, the school had announced a few days earlier that there would be an additional holiday that Thanksgiving.

The secretary smiled as she headed toward the nearby administration building where she was to pick up some papers for the dean. What, she wondered, should she do with the extra time off? And with the extra money in her paycheck each month?

She was still thanking her good luck when she stepped through the double doors of the building. It was a noisy place, she remembered thinking, full of students and faculty changing classes. She waved to a couple of professors, then disappeared into a room off to the right of the hallway.

Moments after Mrs. Baterbaugh closed the door behind her, she knew something was wrong. First, there was the strange, unnaturally powerful odor—like mildewed books and rotting grass. Then she was struck by the silence, a total absence of any kind of noise. It was as if she had suddenly lost her hearing or somehow stumbled into a soundless universe.

"As I entered the room," she later wrote, "everything was quite normal. About four steps into the room was where the strong odor hit me. When I say strong odor, I mean the kind that simply stops you in you tracks and almost chokes you."

It was what she saw, though, that stopped the secretary dead in her tracks.

Mrs. Baterbaugh suddenly became aware of a presence in the otherwise empty room. Not only did she feel chilled by the unexpected presence, the noise outside in the hallway had mysteriously disappeared.

"Everything was deathly quiet," she said. "I looked up and something drew my eyes to the cabinet along the wall in the next room. I looked up again and there she was. She had her back to me, reaching up into one of the shelves of the cabinet with her right hand, and standing perfectly still."

Immediately the secretary sensed that something was markedly out of the ordinary here. The unfamiliar woman standing before her didn't seem to be moving at all—it was as if she were transfixed on the spot, frozen in time. Equally unsettling was the realization that the strange figure was not aware of Mrs. Baterbaugh's presence.

"While I was watching her she never once moved. She was not transparent, and yet I knew she wasn't real. While I was looking at her she just faded away—not parts of her body one at a time, but her whole body all at once."

Shocked by the disturbing vision, Mrs. Baterbaugh stumbled backward, anxious to flee the room. Her most troubling experience was yet to come.

"I am not sure whether I ran or walked over to the window...When I looked out that window there wasn't one modern thing out there. The street [Madison Street] which is less than a half block away from the building wasn't even there, and neither was the new Willard House."

There were people, though—but not any people she knew.

"These people were not in my time," the terrified secretary recalled. "I was back in their time."

Moments before, she had seen a ghost. Now she was looking through a window into the past!

Mrs. Baterbaugh turned from the window and raced back to the door, not daring to think about the ghost or sights outside the window. She had to get away from there—fast.

She reached the door, flung it open wide, and raced out into the hallway, half expecting to run into people wearing hoop skirts and other old-fashioned attire such as she had seen out the window.

Instead she saw students and professors, some of whom she recognized, all mercifully clad in modern clothes. The hallway was the same, too—even the smells were familiar.

The secretary closed her eyes for a moment, drinking in the welcome sight and sound of student chatter and nearby musicians warming up their instruments.

Then she walked slowly out of the building, down the steps, and back across campus to the dean's office. She didn't stop until she had told him everything—the silent, strangely-attired people outside the window, the horse-drawn buggies, the old-timey cars.

And, of course, the specter of the strange woman in the archives room.

Ghosts.

Horses and buggies.

What did it mean?

Somehow she had slipped back into another time, and she was scared—more scared than she had ever been in her life.

Word of Mrs. Baterbaugh's experience quickly spread across campus. Eventually, someone on the staff suggested that the figure in Mrs. Baterbaugh's vision closely resembled a former music teacher at the school.

Only problem was, *that* teacher was dead—had been since 1936. She had died in the same room where Mrs. Baterbaugh had undergone her strange experience. Those who listened to Mrs. Baterbaugh's description of the uncanny vision swore it was the same teacher.

But how could it have been?

By all accounts, Mrs. Baterbaugh had experienced something known in paranormal circles as retrocognition, a term applied to "seeing" a person or landscape belonging to the past. Countless thousands of "ghost stories" have been reported and investigated down through the centuries, but cases involving "phantom scenery" are reportedly a rare and puzzling phenomena not well known to the general public.

That's because few authenticated accounts of such experiences are available to psychic researchers. Whenever reports of "visionary landscapes" do occur, they are usually given first-class treatment by investigators of the paranormal.

Mrs. Baterbaugh had not only seen a ghost, she apparently had also witnessed a phantom landscape from the past.

Another astounding case of retrocognition involving phantom scenery was reported by a columnist with the Dearborn, Michigan, *Press* on May 10, 1973. The columnist, Joyce Hagelthorn, told how Laura Jean Daniels of Dearborn was walking home from work late one night when suddenly the familiar urban surroundings simply vanished.

One moment she had been walking along, gazing up at the moon. The next, everything—houses, automobiles, lampposts, garbage bins, fences, and streets—was gone.

"Even the pavement on the sidewalk was gone," Daniels told Haglethorn. "And I [was] walking down a brick path."

The frightened woman added, there "were no houses on either side of me, but several hundred feet before me was a thatched-roof cottage—-there was a heavy scent of roses and honeysuckle in the air."

As she strolled up the brick path and drew closer to the cottage, she noticed a couple of people sitting in the garden, a man and a woman, in very old-fashioned clothes. There were obviously in love, she said, because they were embracing, and she could see the expression on the woman's face.

A small dog then shot out toward her, barking.

"He was quivering all over. The man looked up and called to the dog to stop barking. I somehow realized that he couldn't see me, and yet I could smell the flowers and feel the gate beneath my hand. While I was trying to make up my mind what to do, I turned to look back the way I had just come, and there was my street!"

Even then, she could still feel the gate in her hands. But when she turned for another peek at the cottage, it had vanished.

"It was gone and I was standing right in the middle of my own block, just a few doors from home. The cottage, the lovers, and the wee dog were gone."

Assuming that some portion of what victims of retrocognition claim to have seen is true, what are we to make of their experiences? Many psychic investigators believe such incidents can happen, and *do* happen—more examples, they say, of the mysterious powers of the mind which science is only now beginning to understand.

Tears From Heaven

LATE NIGHT PHONE CALLS were nothing new to the Reverend George Papadeas. As the busy pastor of St. Paul's Greek Orthodox Church in Hampstead, New York, he was used to having his sleep interrupted in the wee hours by distraught parishioners in need of guidance.

But when the phone rang on the night of March 16, 1960, Papadeas was in no mood to talk. He had just turned off the light and crawled into bed, desperate for a few hours of badly needed sleep.

Dutifully, however, he reached over and picked up the phone.

"Father," the young woman's voice pleaded on the other end of the line. "You must come over and see the miracle."

Papadeas recognized the voice instantly. It was Pagona Catsounis, wife of Pagionitis Catsounis. They were both devout members of his church.

"Miracle?" the minister grumbled. "What kind of miracle do you mean, Pagona?"

"It's the Blessed Virgin," Pagona stammered. "She is weeping."

For the next couple of minutes, Papadeas listened attentively while the young housewife recounted one of the strangest stories the minister had ever heard. Apparently the woman had gone into her living room to pray, as she did every night, to the small icon of the Holy Mother hanging on the wall above her sofa.

While she knelt, she noticed something wet and glistening on the six-by-eight-inch colored icon reproduction. When she looked closer, she realized it was tears—tears streaming down the Blessed Virgin's face!

When her husband heard her screams, he rushed into the room and saw the tears, too. They both decided to phone the priest for advice.

In his time, Papadeas had dealt with some pretty bizarre cases, ranging from adultery and murder to divorce and suicide. On a couple of occasions he had even performed the ancient ritual of exorcism. Never had the bearded, Greek-born pastor faced a crisis he couldn't handle.

But a *weeping* Madonna?

"It's really happening, Father," Pagona persisted. "Even as I speak, her tears cover the picture."

"Are you sure of what you see?" the priest asked.

"You must see for yourself," the twenty-two-year-old parishioner replied, begging him to come at once.

As a man of the cloth, Papadeas had been well-trained in the study of miracles. That didn't mean he *believed* in them necessarily, and on the way over to the Catsounis house that night he wondered what unsettling event had caused the couple to think they had experienced a miracle.

When Papadeas arrived at their modest apartment in Island Park, he was greeted not only by the emotional husband and wife, but also by two other members of the congregation, whose astonishing radiance made him feel uncomfortable. Something inside him whispered: *They have seen the face of God!*

Without saying a word, Pagona Catsounis pointed to the small, brightly colored icon. There was nothing extraordinary about the artifact; Papadeas, who had seen thousands of such adornments in the homes and apartments of his parishioners over the years, thought it looked very ordinary indeed.

But when he looked closer at this one hanging over the sofa, his eyes suddenly grew wide.

There were tears—unmistakable tears—welling up in the Blessed Virgin's left eye.

"When I arrived," he later wrote, "a tear was drying beneath the left eye. Then just before the devotions ended, I saw another tear well in her eye."

He said the tear "started as a small, round globule of moisture in the corner of her left eye, and it slowly trickled down her face."

As far as the minister was concerned, he had witnessed a true miracle.

When news leaked out the next day about the miraculous event, thousands of visitors began descending on the Catsounis household to witness the miracle for themselves. The "blessed event" was well publicized by newspapers and radio stations throughout the city.

To the delight of the crowds, the Virgin continued to shed copious tears, often in full view of witnesses. On March 23, seven days after Pagona had first noticed the tears, the icon was taken to St. Paul's for safekeeping and to give the Catsounises some much-needed relief from the publicity.

By then, the weeping had all but ceased, yet thousands of other visitors flocked to the church daily for a glimpse of the Blessed Virgin, whose picture had been enshrined on the altar.

Miracle or not, many of those who came to St. Paul's sincerely believed they had witnessed some kind of divine apparition. Their unwavering conviction was not unlike that of millions of others around the world whose visionary claims continue to tug at the mystical fabric of the Church.

In 1989, for example, a similar phenomenon was reported at the Holy Trinity Catholic Church in Ambridge, Pennsylvania. The incident, which made international news, centered around a life-size statue of Jesus Christ that allegedly closed its eyes during a Good Friday service.

That same year, thousands of worshippers in Lubbock, Texas, saw visions of Mary in the sky above St. John Neumann Catholic Church.

One of the most widely publicized visions of a religious figure occurred in 1932 when the "clearly discernible" figure of Christ appeared in a marble wall inside St. Bartholomew's Church in New York City. The miracle was discovered by the rector, the Reverend Dr. Robert Norwood, a few seconds after completing a Lenten talk on "The Mystery of Incarnation."

"I happened to glance at the sanctuary wall and was amazed to see this lovely figure of Christ in the marble," the reverend was quoted as saying. "I had never noticed it before. As it seemed to me to be an actual expression on the face of the marble of what I was preaching, 'His Glorious Body.' I consider it a curious and beautiful happening."

Norwood said the figure was about one-and-a-half feet tall and was well delineated in the marble directly above the sanctuary door. The figure was clad in white robes and appeared to be emerging from a tomb hewn in a rock. A primitive cross was visible in the background, he said.

In an interview with *The New York Times*, Norwood offered his own theory about the miracle:

"I have a weird theory that the force of thought, a dominant thought, may be strong and powerful enough to be somehow transferred to stone in its receptive state. How this Christ-like figure came to be there, of course, I don't know."

He concluded with a question. "Is thought the power of life? People can scoff, but the figure is there."

Throughout the world, visions such as those described above seem to have been on the increase since Norwood's claim. One theologian estimates about two hundred have been recorded in the last six decades alone. Most have been dismissed as hallucinations, illusions, and outright fraud, yet the Catholic Church counts fourteen apparitions as "worthy of pious belief."

Leonore Piper's Amazing Gift

TOWARD THE END OF THE last century, newspapers in America and abroad were full of stories about individuals who claimed to have psychic powers enabling them to tap into the unseen spirit world.

In places like Boston and New York, London and Paris, séances became a fashionable pastime, especially among the upper crust of society. Just about every lady and gentleman of any standing had his or her own personal medium—a so-called "guide" who, for a fee, would help them establish contact with a deceased relative or friend.

One of the most remarkable of such mediums was a frail young housewife named Leonore Piper. Over the years, hundreds of visitors flocked to her tidy townhouse on the outskirts of Boston for a reading. These included scientists and theologians and other clairvoyants and psychics anxious to learn more about the possibility of life after death.

In her day, Mrs. Piper—who rarely spoke above a whisper—entertained and enthralled some of the most respectable citizens in America and England. Her fame as a medium rivaled even that of the notorious Fox Sisters of New York.

As psychics went, Mrs. Piper seemed to be the best. And the most honest. Teams of investigators, including one led by the brilliant Harvard scientist William James, were convinced the shy Bostonion possessed genuine paranormal ability.

After a lengthy study of her mediumistic powers, Dr. James—whose wife had attended sessions with Mrs. Piper on several occasions—made the following observation:

"My impression…was that Mrs. P. was either possessed of supernormal powers or knew the members of my wife's family by sight and had by some lucky coincidence become acquainted with such a multitude of their domestic circumstances as to produce the startling impression which she did. My later knowledge of her sittings and personal acquaintance with her has led me to absolutely reject the latter explanation, and to believe that she has supernormal powers."

The professor was so impressed with Mrs. Piper's mysterious powers that he personally arranged readings for the next eighteen months. His investigation left him with the conclusion that "most of the phenomena of psychical research are rooted in reality."

Eventually word reached Dr. Richard Hodgson, director of the Society for Psychical Research in London, about Mrs. Piper's uncanny mediumistic powers. Not only was Hodgson one of the Society's most outspoken leaders, he was also one of its most skeptical. A few years earlier, he had led a personal investigation of Madam Blavatsky that ended in the famous founder of theosophy being exposed as a fraud.

The dapper scientist, who always dressed in Edwardian style, was convinced that "nearly all professional mediums form a gang of vulgar tricksters." He believed most of them were in cahoots with each other, and vowed to use the full force of the Society for Psychical Research to expose them wherever possible and wipe them out.

As soon as he accepted the investigation, he put detectives on the trail of Mrs. Piper and other members of her family. No evidence turned up, however, to suggest that the medium obtained information about her clients in any way to her advantage.

Still not convinced that her powers were real, Dr. Hodgson started "planting" customers. One such customer, James Hyslop, professor of logic and ethics at Columbia University, even wore a mask and used a pseudonym during his first two or three séances with Mrs. Piper.

Despite such extraordinary precautions, Mrs. Piper succeeded in providing the professor with outstanding evidence which purported to come from the spirit world. After twelve sessions with Mrs. Piper, Hyslop—who previously did not believe in life after death—became convinced that he had, indeed, been communicating with friends and relatives who had long since died.

Dr. Hodgson, satisfied that fraud was not the answer to the Piper phenomenon, refused to accept that spirits of the dead were communicating through the medium. There had to be some other answer, perhaps a subconscious explanation. Even Mrs. Piper did not insist that the messages she received from beyond were from ghosts or spirits.

"Spirits of the dead may have controlled me and they may not," she said. "I confess that I do not know."

At the beginning of each reading, Mrs. Piper would reportedly slip into a deep trance from which she wouldn't move and in which she was oblivious to physical sensation or pain. Professor James noted that her lips barely moved while conversing with otherworldly communicants. He also made a small incision in her wrist which did not bleed while she was entranced. Afterward, the wound bled freely and the scar remained with her for life.

Another investigator, Sir Oliver Lodge, once pushed a needle into her hand to determine her state of consciousness. Not a muscle flinched. Another researcher, a French doctor named Charles Richet, pushed a feather up her nostril to monitor her response. The result was the same: not a twitch or indication of any kind that the slumbering medium was conscious.

After being poked, sliced, tickled, and ridiculed for so many years, why did Mrs. Piper—who made very little money from her séances—tolerate such treatment?

"When I found that I possessed a gift, power, or what you will, which to the best of my knowledge formed no part of my conscious Self, I determined then that I would give my life, if need be, in the attempt to fathom its true nature."

Until her death after the turn of the century, Mrs. Piper continued to hold séances and offer hope to her troubled sitters. Many people continued to call her a fraud even though no evidence was ever found to substantiate such claims.

A few months before she died, Mrs. Piper offered an additional observation about her amazing powers as a psychic medium: "I wonder...after all this time [whether] we are any nearer the real solution than we were in the beginning."

"...and Every Creeping Thing"

The Phantom Ape-Man of the Northwest

FOR THE PAST COUPLE OF decades or so, Professor Grover Krantz has combed the mist-shrouded wilds of the Pacific Northwest in search of an elusive creature that hundreds of people have seen, but few believe exists.

Krantz's lonely quest has brought him disappointment and no small measure of ridicule. Still the bearded, bespectacled anthropologist presses on, month after month, year after year, chasing down leads and interviewing eyewitnesses who claim to have encountered what he calls *Gigantopithecus blacki*, or Bigfoot, the legendary ape-man that supposedly stalks remote regions of North America from Florida to Alaska.

Though he has never seen one himself, the Washington State University professor passionately believes that between two hundred and two thousand such monsters inhabit the remote forests and rugged high country of northern California, Oregon, Washington, and British Columbia. Smaller populations probably inhabit the lonely swamps and bayous of several southern states, he thinks, as well as certain sections of New England and the Great Lakes.

Krantz is not alone in his belief in Bigfoot. A growing number of respected scientists in the United States and Canada believe that some kind of giant, hairy primate haunts out-of-the-way locations in North America. Known as the Sasquatch in Canada and the Skunk-Ape in Florida's

Everglades, the creature is often described as foul-smelling, averaging eight feet in height, and weighing approximately one thousand pounds.

Unlike the fanatical amateurs who dominate the Bigfoot scene, Krantz is a sensible and methodical scientist, known for his uncompromising insistence on empirical evidence in the field as well as in the laboratory. He cuts no corners in examining data and his reputation as a gruelling interrogator is legendary.

"If science accepted every creature on the testimony of ten or so sightings," he says, "then we would have a zoological inventory that included unicorns, goblins, griffins, fairies, and moth-men. But on the other hand, if even just one Sasquatch story is true, then the animal is real and the species is there."

Krantz, who personally has investigated about one thousand reported sightings—of which more than half have been dismissed as fraud, mistaken identity, or "reflections from the bottom of a bottle"—maintains a large collection of Bigfoot prints in his laboratory, and believes the actual number of sightings may be "ten times" that many.

"Most witnesses tell very few people about what they saw," he pointed out in an interview.

While few scholars have risked their careers and reputations so unabashedly as has Krantz in his pursuit of the phantom ape-man, some, like Dr. John Napier, author and former director of primate biology at the Smithsonian Institution, are convinced that Bigfoot is more than a fairytale.

"I am convinced the Sasquatch exists," Napier was quoted as saying. "There is too much evidence to suggest otherwise."

Stories about a Bigfoot-like creature existed long before the arrival of white explorers in the 16th and 17th centuries. According to anthropologist Thomas Buckley, various groups of Indians, including the Karok, developed legends about "upslope persons"—large, hairy, strong, stupid, and crude men-beasts that apparently were early versions of Bigfoot.

It is Buckley's belief that those hairy giants in Indian mythology were the forerunners of today's Bigfoot.

One of the first documented encounters with the man-beast was recounted by none other than America's own big-game-hunter-turned-president, Theodore Roosevelt. In his book *Wilderness Hunter,* Roosevelt tells the hair-raising "true" story about a couple of hunters in the mid-1800s who apparently had a run-in with something resembling Bigfoot.

According to Roosevelt, a man named Baumann and a fellow trapper were camping in the Northwest woods when they came across some large tracks. Thinking they had been made by a bear, the trappers set off for work in the woods and soon forgot about them. That evening when they returned, they found the camp torn apart.

"At midnight," Roosevelt wrote, "Baumann was awakened by some noise and sat up in his blankets. As he did so his nostrils were struck by a strong wild-beast odor and he caught the loom of a great body in the darkness at the mouth of the lean-to."

Baumann grabbed his rifle and fired at the vague, threatening shadow. "He must have missed, for immediately afterwards he heard the smashing of the underwood as the thing, whatever it was, rushed off into the impenetrable blackness of the forest and night."

Unnerved by the experience, the men built up the fire and huddled beside it until dawn. Later, their confidence renewed in the broad glare of daylight, the men decided to split their chores—Baumann set off to check the remaining traps in the woods, and his companion started packing.

When Baumann returned, "his eyes fell on the body of his friend, stretched beside the trunk of a great fallen spruce. Rushing towards it the horrified trapper found that the body was still warm, but that the neck was broken, while there were four great fang marks in the throat."

Roosevelt added, "The footprints of the unknown beast, printed deep in the soft soil, told the whole story.... It had not eaten the body, but apparently had romped and gambolled around it in uncouth and ferocious glee, occasionally rolling it over and over; and had then fled back into the soundless depths of the woods."

The future president did not say what he thought the creature was that killed Baumann's friend. Many readers of his account have wondered whether the thing that mutilated the trapper could in fact have been a Bigfoot.

Over the years, thousands of footprints attributed to the evasive creature have been found, but so far not Bigfoot himself. Droppings and traces of hair have been discovered aplenty on trees, fences, and even on the bumpers of cars—but no bodies or bones.

The remarkable thing is that most of the people who claim to have seen Bigfoot swear they are telling the truth. Scientist and author Ivan T. Sanderson has no trouble accepting a large number of the Bigfoot-sighting stories. He is firmly convinced that some kind of primitive, human-like animal inhabits remote regions of the modern world.

Sanderson has classified such creatures into three categories—the *Neanderthaler,* or caveman type, found in the Far East; Bigfoot or Sasquatch, which roams North America, Central America, and possibly South America; and *Meh-Teh,* a human-sized creature with twelve-inch fangs known as the Abominable Snowman of the Himalaya Mountains.

If Bigfoot does exist in North America, it has plenty of elbow room. Its primary range—northern California, Oregon, Washington, and British Columbia—covers more than 125,000 square miles of thick forest and rugged high country. In his book *The Search for Bigfoot,* Peter Byrne writes that there are deep ravines in the region "that never hear the voice of Man."

Francis Hitching, author of *The Mysterious World: An Atlas of the Unexplained,* agrees: "Odd though it may seem, the coniferous mountain forests of the North American continent are largely unexplored, and there is no compelling reason why a quite large population of unknown beasts should not exist there, surviving on a frugal and mostly vegetarian diet."

Why hasn't conclusive evidence been forthcoming? Where are the pictures? Where are the remains? Where are the captured specimens?

Some experts in the field suggest that Bigfoot, like other wild animals of the forest, bury their dead deep in the ground. Fast-acting acid soils at such depths account for the fact that no fossils have been found, notes Peter Byrne. In addition, the author says, a "natural disposal system operates in Bigfoot's North American area. It consists of crows and ravens, buzzards, and other meat-eating birds." Add to that list other carnivores and scavengers like coyotes, wolves, foxes, various rodents, porcupines, and even bears, and the complete disposition of Bigfoot bones becomes clear. "Everything is eaten," says Byrne, "even the antlers of big buck deer."

Assuming, then, that populations of Bigfoot do exist, two natural questions arise—what are they and where did they come from?

Theories abound, of course, but one links them to giant ancestors of human beings who at some remote time mated with huge apes and produced a new breed. Another explanation, offered by author Alan Landsburg, is that millions of years ago, apes mated with evolving humans, and the offspring wandered off into high country where they wouldn't have to compete for food and other necessities.

Still another idea, only slightly more fanciful, holds that aliens from outer space planted the Bigfoot creatures on earth for observation or some other reason. Such an origin would make them less than human, of course, thereby easing a moral dilemma for those who argue that shooting or killing a Bigfoot would be justified in the name of science.

Scientist Jon E. Beckjord of Seattle does not care for such a cruel rationalization one bit.

"Because these reports feature hairy bodies, and not hairless bodies," he charged, "we have persons who feel this is license to shoot first and ask questions afterward. I deplore this form of…arrogance."

But Krantz argues that the only way to truly establish the reality of Bigfoot "is to go out and shoot" one. That's okay, he says, "because nothing indicates that it's human. No dependable Sasquatch report shows any sign of its using or making tools, communicating information by language, or being part of a social group. So it's an animal."

If he had the funds, Krantz said he would hire a dozen or so big-game hunters and march them off into the high country of the Pacific Northwest with instructions not to come back without a trophy.

"I'm convinced they could do it within five years," he said in an interview.

And what if his hunters get lucky?

"It would mean that science has completely missed one of the biggest and potentially most important mammalian species on Earth," he says. "But perhaps the most critical effect of such a find would be on an emotional level. If this is what I think it is, it's the closest living relative of human beings, closer than the great apes. That would make it the biological discovery of the century."

The Gloucester Monster

BETWEEN THE HOURS OF four and five o'clock on the afternoon of August 14, 1817, Matthew Gaffney was rowing his small craft across the main harbor at Gloucester, Massachusets. He happened to notice an unusual disturbance in the water about a hundred yards away.

Something huge seemed to be churning beneath the gray waters, and from all indications appeared to be on the verge of breaking through the boiling surface any moment.

Intrigued, the fisherman paddled nearer.

Seconds later, an enormous marine animal resembling a sea serpent shot through the waves, belching and hissing, then launched itself in the direction of Gaffney. The monster's triangular head appeared fully as large as a four-gallon keg and its body as big around as a barrel.

Gaffney had never seen anything like it before in his life. Like most other fishermen in the area, he had heard the usual tavern tales about sea serpents and such but until today had dismissed them as nothing more than rumors and foolish old salts' tales.

As he watched the strange animal swim closer to his boat, he suddenly felt afraid. The thing was big—bigger than any fish he'd ever seen in these waters, including whales. It moved fast, too, and that's what disturbed Gaffney most.

When the creature had drawn to within thirty feet of the boat, it finally halted—not for long, but long enough for Gaffney to observe its markings and dimensions. The best he could tell, the animal was about forty feet in length. It had a dark-colored head, and the underpart of its massive snout and several feet of its belly were almost white.

The frightened fisherman decided he'd seen enough. He pulled out his gun, fired once at the monster, and started rowing toward shore as fast as he could.

Instead of retreating, the enraged animal charged straight for the boat. Gaffney rowed hard, but there was no way he could hope to outrun the creature behind him. He did the only thing he could—he closed his eyes and braced for the worst.

Then a miracle happened. When the monster had drawn to within a few feet of the boat, it suddenly dived beneath the keel, resurfaced about a hundred yards away, and then disappeared.

Gaffney spent the rest of the afternoon at a bar telling anyone who would listen about his chilling experience in the harbor. Nobody believed him. A few days later, more reports started coming in about a sea monster prowling the gloomy harbor.

Shipmaster Solomon Allen III signed a sworn statement that he, too, had seen such a creature in the same vicinity. Allen's description matched other accounts, except in his case, the creature appeared to be about ninety feet long, and its head resembled that of a rattlesnake.

So many sea monster sightings came in over the next few days that local authorities formed a special commission in Boston to study the reports. Within a week, the three-member panel had compiled an impressive number of sworn statements from others who claimed such encounters. Doctors, sea captains, businessmen, clergymen, and military officers were counted among those who confessed to having seen a sea serpent in the vicinity of Gloucester in recent days.

Later that month, two women watched in horror as a "sea monster" swam into Cape Ann harbor, which lies just north of Gloucester. That event was also witnessed by several fishermen. The next week, a seaman named Amos Story saw another marine beast enter Gloucester harbor. That sighting was followed by yet another, during which twenty more people—including Mr. London Nash, justice of the peace for

Gloucester—watched a similar creature cavort in the harbor for about half an hour.

Newspapers and magazines were quick to pick up on the stories, of course, flooding their front pages and feature sections with interviews and news about the latest wave of sightings. The *Salem Gazette*, the *Boston Daily Advertiser*, the *Salem Register*, and *Philadelphia Magazine* were only four of many publications billing the Gloucester sea serpent as "the largest ever seen in America."

According to the *Gazette*, the creature was seen "playing sometimes within fifteen or twenty feet of the shore, affording a better opportunity to observe him than had before occurred. Gentlemen from Gloucester...state that he appeared to them even of greater magnitude than had before been represented, and should judge from their own observation that he was as much as one hundred fifty feet in length and as big around as a barrel."

Such reports, especially one stating the creature had "an enormous mouth," kept mariners from venturing too far out into the harbor. Others, however, anxious to capture or kill the unusual animal, armed themselves with muskets, harpoons, and axes and patrolled the inlet day and night.

Several hunters were able to get off a few rounds at the creature, but it always managed to elude either death or capture. There were a number of hair-raising encounters, but no reports exist of any attacks on or casualties among humans.

The first man to be interrogated by authorities about his claims was Amos Story. In his appearance before the Linnean Society of Boston—the special committee formed to investigate the sightings—Story said:

"I saw a strange marine animal, that I believe to be a serpent, at the southward and eastward end of Ten Pound Island, in the harbor of said Gloucester. It was between the hours of ten and one o'clock when I first saw him, and he continued in sight for an hour and a half. I was sitting on the shore and was about twenty rods [three hundred thirty feet] from him when he was the nearest to me."

Story said the creature's head "appeared shaped much like the head of the sea-turtle," and that it "carried his head from ten to twelve inches above the surface of the water. His head at that distance appeared larger than the head of any dog that I ever saw."

The serpent "moved very rapidly through the water," Story continued, "I should say a mile in two, or at most, in three minutes. I saw no bunches on his back. On this day I did not see more than ten or twelve feet of his rough and scaly body."

In the days and weeks following the panel's investigation, still more sightings of the Gloucester monster continued to pour in. On one ship, the captain and his entire crew watched the creature pass within close range. A few days later, another ship moved within an oar's length of the monster.

In his definitive study of the subject, James B. Sweeney concluded that what had been seen "was indeed a transient sea monster" that frequented Gloucester's harbor from time to time from August 1 until August 23. Upon leaving the Gloucester area, Sweeney noted "it was again seen heading in a northerly direction on August 28; however, it was observed on October 3 and 5 in Long Island Sound."

The creature never returned to Gloucester, though a number of unreliable reports of sightings continued to trickle in over the years.

Behemoth in the New World

WHEN THE FIRST EUROPEANS came to the New World, they heard stories about terrifying beasts and giant men that once populated the vast wilderness.

Most of these stories were dismissed as superstitious prattle. But as settlers pushed westward into the thick woods and unexplored mountains of Appalachia they began to make startling discoveries. Along riverbanks and hillsides and littering the untrod forest floor were bones—enormous bones, larger than any they'd ever seen before.

In time, as more and more bones were unearthed, many people came to believe there might be something to the old Indian legends after all. What else could account for such abominations in nature? Surely, they reasoned, at some remote time in the past, there had lived an ancient race of men—"super men," the Indians called them—whose primeval world shook beneath the thunderous hoofbeats of their mortal enemies, the great five-legged monsters of legend.

If anyone doubted it, all he had to do was examine the evidence in the ground—tons and tons of huge fossilized bones, scattered from the rocky coasts of Maine to the windswept plains of Texas, the remains of those who had come before.

Even Cortés, traveling in Mexico in 1519, had encountered tremendous bones that could only have belonged to monsters and giants that had obviously lived long before the Deluge. In 1705, more colossal bones were found, this time in New York State. "Bone fever" was starting to grip the colonies.

Similar fossils began turning up throughout eastern North America with greater frequency. One important discovery was made in 1739 by the Baron de Longueuil, an officer in the French army, who came upon a deposit of large bones and teeth while on a military mission in Ohio. One year later, another large find was located in Boone County, Kentucky, at a place called Big Bone Lick.

When John Bartram, one of America's most famous naturalists, heard of the Kentucky bones, he sent his friend James Wright to investigate. In 1762, Wright traveled into Shawnee country and, in the course of his inquiry, asked whether any of these large creatures had ever been seen alive.

"They answered," he told Bartram, "they had never heard them spoken of, other than as in the condition they are at present, nor ever heard of any such creature having been seen by the oldest man, or his father."

But according to an old Shawnee tradition, long ago there had lived men as big as the great beasts, who hunted them, slew them, and slung them over their backs "as an Indian now does a deer. When there were no more of these strong men left alive," said the Shawnees, "God killed these mighty creatures, that they should not hurt the present race of Indians."

With the discovery of enigmatic earthen mounds in the Mississippi Valley and southeastern states, the mystery only intensified. Many colonists believed these colossal artificial hills—some of them larger that the pyramids of Egypt and stoneworks of Mexico—had been built by none other than the vanished race of giants countless eons ago.

Yet another mystery fired the imagination of scientists and thinking men everywhere: if such men and creatures had once existed, could survivors still not inhabit the unknown lands west of the mountains?

A certain Virginia gentleman named Thomas Jefferson, whose wide-ranging mind was attuned to many forms of learning, would soon become obsessed with trying to find the answer to that question. Like many scientists and thinkers of his day, the future president of the United States believed the giant bones were the remains of elephant-like creatures called mammoths—not some super race of human beings lost in the dimness of time.

To support his theory, Jefferson collected Indian traditions concerning the existence of a giant carnivorous animal with elephant-like features. An Algonquin tribe told of a "mighty animal...with an arm coming out of its shoulder" and of another beast that left "large round tracks in the snow" and "struck its enemies with its long nose."

The Chitimacha Indians of Louisiana believed that "a long time ago a being with a long nose came out of the ocean and began to kill people. It would root up trees with its nose to get at people who sought refuge in the branches." A myth of the Penobscot Indians told of "moving hills without vegetation" that turned out to be, on close inspection, "great animals with long teeth, animals so huge that when they lay down they could not get up."

Other Indians related legends about how the great beasts were driven into a distant land by God after the giants had all died off. Could that distant land be the unexplored wilderness beyond the Appalachian Mountains?

Despite such reports, American explorers failed to find mammoths anywhere as they cautiously moved westward in the 18th century.

Jefferson refused to believe they were extinct. The very idea that a species could become extinct went against Jefferson's philosophical convictions. As a believer in the "great chain of being," he declared that the "intelligent and powerful Agent" that directed the universe would not permit it to be "reduced to a shapeless chaos" by the extinction of a species.

In Jefferson's mind the great beasts—which he called American mammoths—still lived in remote northern parts of the continent. Since the animal was carnivorous, he reasoned that it might have retreated to such regions as encroaching civilization continued to wipe out big game, its source of food.

After America's acquisition of 800,000 square miles of trans-Mississippi territory in 1803, Jefferson sent teams of explorers out with instructions to "find live mammoths." He insisted that "in the present interior of our continent there is surely space enough" for such creatures.

Although they found many bones—and more tales about giant, shaggy beasts stalking the northern forests—explorers Meriwether Lewis and William Clark returned in 1806 with the disappointing news that they had not seen a single mammoth alive anywhere.

As recent archaeology indicates, it is quite likely that mammoths and their look-alike cousins, the mastodons, survived in North America until a few thousand years ago. No reliable date more recent than 11,000 years ago has been forthcoming, but there is some Carbon 14 evidence at a site in Washtenaw County, Michigan, suggesting an age of between 6,000 and 6,500 years.

It is theoretically possible that mastodons or mammoths continued to range certain parts of the United States until five or six thousand years ago, when they might finally have been driven into extinction by Stone Age people. Despite all the rumors and legends, it seems safe to conclude that the five-legged monsters of yore have been missing from the American landscape for many thousands of years.

Giants in the Earth

LATE ONE AFTERNOON IN October, 1869, workmen digging a well on the outskirts of an obscure little village in upstate New York were startled when their shovels uncovered what appeared to be the mummified remains of a large human foot.

Digging deeper, the workmen found that the enormous foot was attached to the body of an incredibly large man, measuring more than ten feet tall and weighing nearly three thousand pounds. Apparently the giant had been dead a very long time—thousands of years, perhaps.

In those days, newspapers were full of the latest findings of the naturalist, Charles Darwin. People everywhere were talking about them. Could it be, some residents of Cardiff wondered, that this mysterious creature from the past was the so-called "missing link" in man's evolution?

Others turned to the Bible for answers. At least one fundamentalist minister believed that the human behemoth was proof that an ancient race of giants had lived on the earth long before the Flood. "There were giants in the earth in those days," the book of Genesis says.

William C. Newell, the Cardiff farmer on whose land the giant had been found, was stunned by all the publicity and scientific curiosity surrounding the discovery. Even so, when strangers as well as a steady stream of neighbors kept swarming onto his property to see the giant with their own eyes, Newell's entrepreneurial instincts quickly took command.

He erected a tent over the giant's grave, and for fifty cents, the public was treated to a fifteen-minute viewing and a lecture on what the barkers called the latest and perhaps the most remarkable of all the wonders of the Americas. Thousands of visitors, some from as far away as Europe, came to see the Cardiff Giant, and soon Newell was a wealthy man.

Cardiff became a boom town. Hotels overflowed with visitors and local restaurants had to add on extra rooms and tables. When Newell took his giant to nearby Syracuse for a show, every hotel in town was booked.

Among the visitors who came to gawk were scientists, some of whom were convinced the giant truly belonged to a long-forgotten race of man. Some were calling him the original man. One investigator so firmly believed the giant to be real, he announced that any man who declared it to be a hoax "simply declared himself a fool."

Medical doctors who examined the creature also insisted the giant had once been a living human being. To prove his point, one doctor drilled a hole in the giant's enormous skull and claimed that he was able to make out fascinating aspects of the giant's anatomy.

Finally, even as the Cardiff Giant continued to make headlines around the world, a cousin of Newell's stepped forward and announced it was all a hoax. George Hull, a cigar manufacturer from Syracuse, had hatched the scheme for the sole purpose of getting even with a fundamentalist preacher named Turk with whom he had recently been arguing over the biblical origins of man.

Hull decided to teach Turk a lesson. He bought a large block of stone in Fort Dodge, Iowa, and then transported it to Chicago where he hired a crew of sculptors to fashion it into the likeness of a giant human being. To make it look authentic, the sculptors—who worked in sworn secrecy—inserted hundreds of large darning needles into a block of wood before hammering it all over the body to simulate the pores of the skin.

Finally, after dousing the giant with sulfuric acid to make it look old, Hull had it transported secretly to Newell's farm. where it was buried by night to await the great moment of discovery.

Hull couldn't have orchestrated the hoax any better than he did. As soon as the ministers got wind of the find, they descended onto the site to pray and offer thanks to God for opening their eyes to mankind's biblical past.

Of course, Hull and Newell made a lot of money, too, but by the end of the year, the fraud had been pretty well exposed, and the crowds of visitors gradually decreased. Many *still* came, however, to see the famous Cardiff Giant, hoax or not.

So popular was the giant that P.T. Barnum, the world-famous showman, built his own replica of the Cardiff Giant when his offer to purchase the original was turned down.

Although Hull and Newell made a fortune from their hoax, many reputations wee ruined, including those of preachers who had accepted the giant on faith and of numerous scientists who had staked their reputations on its authenticity.

The Incredible Iceman of Minnesota

THE STORY SHE TOLD was terrifying.

There was no particular reason for Helen Westring to feel afraid on that snowy morning in 1966 as she trudged through the icy patch of woods near her home in Bemidji, Minnesota.

She knew the territory well, having hunted and hiked these parts for years. This day she was armed with her favorite high-powered rifle and determined to bring back a trophy regardless of how far into the gloomy forest her mission took her.

Still, she kept a watchful lookout for brown bears. Several attacks had been reported in the area in recent years, and the last thing Helen wanted was a run-in with one of those big critters.

As she pressed deeper into the forest, another worry began to intrude—the possibility of an encounter with Bigfoot. Bigfoot might be just a myth to a lot of people, but Helen and most other folks around Bemidji knew different. Hardly a year went by without at least one sighting of this mysterious creature being reported in the local media.

So preoccupied was she with bears and Bigfoot that Helen didn't notice the large, hairy, pink-eyed monster creeping up behind her. At the last second, she spun around, gun raised, but it was too late. Snarling and howling at the top of its lungs, the thing was on her instantly.

"It was huge and shaggy, a real ugly-looking thing," Helen said years later in a newspaper interview. "It had watery eyes which completely hypnotized me. It was covered with brown and white hair, with a short neck, big hands and long arms."

Helen can't recall exactly what happened next. All she remembers, before passing out, was being dragged to the ground by the creature, and then feeling its hairy body descend on her in lusty fashion. When she came to some time later, she grabbed her rifle and shot dead the beast that had moments before violated her womanhood.

When news of the attack broke, one of the first persons knocking on Helen's door was Frank Hansen, a successful real estate salesman and part-time showman. Not one to miss an opportunity, Hansen proceeded to explain how Helen's harrowing encounter in the north Minnesota woods was going to make them both rich.

Hansen's plan was to encase the dead creature in a block of ice and put it on display at museums and carnivals across the country. People would pay good money to see such a monster, the showman promised, and every newspaper, magazine, and radio and television station in the country would be more than willing to help publicize such an astonishing Ice Age discovery.

They would make millions, the fast-talking showman promised—and he was right.

The "Minnesota Iceman" became an instant hit. For nearly two years, the mysterious monster was hauled from city to city, attracting large crowds at every stop. Newspapers and magazines ran banner headlines whenever the Iceman came to town. Hansen was a favorite guest of the talk show circuit.

From the beginning, Hansen knew that even more interest in the creature could be generated by "doctoring" the facts somewhat. Accordingly, he soon set about billing the creature as the well-preserved corpse of an Ice Age man he had found encased in a six thousand pound block of ice in the Bering Strait. Helen Westring's grim adventure in the woods was quickly forgotten as scores of scientists embraced the possibility that a "missing link" in human evolution had at last been found.

Among those who came to study that creature were the well-known Belgian zoologist Bernard Heuvelmans and his associate, the occult writer and "explorer of the extraordinary," Ivan Sanderson. At first, the two scientists were skeptical about the large, hairy form encased in a block of ice and enclosed in a refrigerated coffin.

After two days of close examination, however, during which time Sanderson made several photos and sketches, Heuvelmans concluded that the monster inside the glass coffin was, indeed, the well-preserved remains of some long-dead ape-like human, probably of Caucasian stock. In a paper published by the Royal Institute of Natural Sciences in Belgium, Heuvelmans wrote of the creature: "It is of fairly normal proportions...but excessively hairy. His skin has the waxlike color characteristic of corpses of men of white race when not tanned by the sun."

Writing in the March 1969 issue of the Belgian Institute of Natural Science bulletin, Heuvelmans said he believed the creature was "a genuine" specimen of the type of *homo sapiens* thought to be living near the Bering Straits either in northernmost Alaska or northeast Asia.

Sightings of such creatures in that part of the world were nothing unusual. For hundreds of years, people as far south as California and as far east as Georgia have reported seeing similar strange, ape-like creatures roaming remote locations. Could this Minnesota Iceman be a Bigfoot, too, a missing link to our evolutionary past?

For a time it seemed as if the Iceman had been accepted as authentic both in popular and academic circles. Then a strange thing happened—whole families of the baffling monster started popping up at carnivals and fairgrounds across the country. Experts and even average show-goers soon began to complain that the creature inside the ice was not the original.

Had cheap, latex copies of the real creature been made in order to increase business?

About the same time, Hansen announced that the real owner of the Iceman was a mysterious millionaire Hollywood moviemaker who wished to remain anonymous. One newspaper quoted Hansen as admitting that the wealthy owner had actually bought the Iceman in a Hong Kong emporium. Before landing in his hands, the creature had been shuttled around the Far East, from Soviet dealers to Japanese whalers to Chinese dealers.

The Hollywood tycoon—whom some newspapermen suspected was the elusive Howard Hughes—was said to be interested only in allowing ordinary people to view their would-be "Neanderthal ancestor."

The conflict over ownership caused scientists at the Smithsonian Institution in Washington, D.C., to reassess their own opinion of the creature. For a while, officials at the institution had tended to believe the claims about the "early man." Then, following the much-publicized squabble over ownership and new allegations that the creature currently on exhibit was not the original Iceman but a latex model instead, the Smithsonian closed the door on further investigation.

Hansen later admitted to the *Rochester Post-Bulletin* that the traveling monster was a fake, a fraud, a man-made illusion. He still insisted that the original Iceman did exist, and that it was being kept on ice at a carefully concealed location.

In the beginning, Hansen stuck to his story, never once wavering. Years later, however, he confessed that he had made up part of the story—the part about Helen Westring having shot the creature after it raped her. In the new version, Hansen swore that he had shot the creature himself while on a hunting trip in northern Minnesota. Afterwards he had kept the body on ice while trying to decide what to do with it.

When he realized the potential profits to be made from such a find, he hired Hollywood special effects technicians to make a copy of the original Iceman, then hid the original in a special climate-controlled environment for protection.

"This was to save wear and tear on the real and original Iceman," Hansen explained. "I then simply switched the exhibits whenever necessary, and talked as fast as I could to fool the press, the public, and the experts."

Somewhere behind Hansen's strange story lies the deep-frozen truth.

In the Midst of Life

Jack Angel's 'Fire From Heaven'

LIFE HAD BEEN KIND TO Jack Angel. The sixty-six year old Georgian was healthy, happily married to a beautiful young woman, and earning a comfortable living as a clothing salesman.

On the night of November 12, 1974, his good luck changed. That's when he pulled his plush motor home—which had been converted into a traveling showroom—into the parking lot of a Savannah motel. His intention was to get a good night's sleep before rising early the next morning to meet several customers.

Before turning in, he phoned his wife to let her know things were fine. Then he pulled back the covers, slipped into his pajamas, and went to sleep.

Four days later, he awoke to an astonishing sight. In the middle of his chest was a large, gaping hole. Then he noticed his right hand—charred black on both sides from the wrist down to his fingers.

"It was just burned, blistered," he later told investigators. "And I had this big explosion in my chest. It left a hell of a hole. I was burned...on my ankle, and up and down my back, in spots."

Incredibly, he felt no pain—only a sore, throbbing sensation in the area of his injuries. Except for the curious hole in his chest and the puzzling burns on his body, Angel appeared to be in perfect health. He was a bit groggy from four days of uninterrupted sleep, but otherwise in remarkable shape.

His first thought was that a fire had somehow broken out in the motor home and scorched his extremities. That theory collapsed, however, when he discovered no other signs of flame in the motor home. It was as if somebody had stuck a blowtorch to various parts of his anatomy without letting the heat touch anything else—not even his pajamas or the sheets on which he lay.

Baffled, but determined to get to the bottom of the mystery, Angel crawled out of bed, showered, and dressed. Nursing his sore right hand, he started across the parking lot to the motel to call his wife. Before he reached the phone, he collapsed and was rushed to Savannah Memorial Hospital.

For Jack Angel, his nightmare was only beginning.

At the hospital, the salesman was informed by doctors that except for the charred hand and wound in his chest there was nothing wrong with him. No evidence of other external injuries. No symptoms of trauma. Nothing.

Angel was mystified.

So were the doctors. Some suspected the salesman had simply made up the story for some reason. Others weren't so sure.

It seemed that whatever had injured the salesman had *come from within*.

"They told me I was burned *internally*," Angel explained. "And he [the doctor] called it a burn."

Unable to get a satisfactory explanation for his injuries from hospital officials, Angel sent his wife to the motor home to look for clues. She found nothing—no faulty wires, malfunctioning electrical appliances, or anything else that could account for his mysterious injuries.

"She couldn't find a thing, not a thing," he said. "No burn spots on the clothing. No evidence of any fire in that bus."

Angel sued the manufacturer of the motor home anyway, insisting that a fire inside the vehicle had somehow caused his injuries. Convinced that an explanation lay somewhere in the wiring, he hired a prestigious Atlanta engineering and law firm with instructions to take the motor home apart in an effort to find out what happened.

After several days of searching, the team of investigators gave up.

The case dragged on for two years, but still no evidence was forthcoming to substantiate Angel's claim. To this day the mystery of Jack Angel's burns remains just that—a mystery.

One man who has a hunch about what happened to Angel is Larry E. Arnold, director of ParaScience International, located in Harrisburg, Pennsylvania.

"Our own conclusion is that Jack burned himself inside," explained Arnold, who has spent years investigating the bizarre and so far unexplained phenomenon known as spontaneous human combustion (SHC).

In cases of SHC, Arnold said, the body's own electrical system "appears to go haywire," sometimes resulting in internal fires that barely singe the skin or any other object around the individual. Sometimes these internal fires can explode, or become so intense the victim is actually cremated, leaving the body in a pile of ashes.

Not much is known about this phenomenon, but for years a lot of people have believed in some unknown power that, under the right circumstances, is capable of igniting internal gases within an individual. Such theories have been used in the past to explain dozens of cases where victims have suddenly, for no apparent reason, burst into flames.

Several books have touched on this peculiar phenomenon, including such popular titles as Herman Melville's *Redburn*, Mark Twain's *Life on the Mississippi*, and Charles Dickens's *Bleak House*. In his study of the subject, *Fire From Heaven*, researcher Michael Harrison sees a connection between SHC and outbreaks of poltergeist activity.

"SHC and poltergeist phenomena imply action and reaction between the 'force generator' and the 'victim,'" Harrison wrote, "the 'force' being the result of deliberate intention, even though the intention may not be consciously known to the human being generating the force."

In most cases of SHC where there has been an investigation, the cause of injury or death has been linked to smoking in bed. However, that rarely explains how a person can be totally consumed in flames without even singeing physical surroundings—bed clothing, furniture, carpets, or walls.

While most medical scientists stop short of accepting SHC as a real phenomenon, Arnold and a few like-minded investigators suspect there may be something to it. It's possible, they say, that some unknown agent inside the body might be responsible for triggering the type of internal infernos that injured Angel and that have reportedly killed and injured scores of victims in the past.

Though he survived his own brush with the unknown, the energetic, once-successful Georgia salesman's ordeal continued. First, his injured arm had to be amputated to prevent infection from spreading. Then his obsession with the case resulted in psychological and financial problems. His wife, unable to cope with his obsession, finally filed for divorce.

Jack Angel's luck had finally run out.

Phantom Booms Off the Carolina Coast

FOR YEARS, RESIDENTS ALONG North Carolina's southeastern shore have reported strange sounds echoing offshore—sounds that cause buildings to shake and windows to rattle.

The sounds come and go without warning. According to some who have heard them, the so-called "Barisal Guns" begin like a low rumble of thunder, and then explode in a final deafening blast.

Nobody knows what causes the sounds—or where they come from—but there are a lot of theories. One of the most frequent explanations is that the "Guns" are actually chunks of the continental shelf dropping off a cliff under the Atlantic Ocean. Others say they are caused by aircraft breaking the sound barrier—even when no aircraft can be confirmed in the area.

Scientists are simply at a loss to explain the phenomenon.

"We have heard it here several times," said Jim Lanier, director of the North Carolina Aquarium at Fort Fisher. "The times we heard it, it was pretty dramatic. It sounds exactly like artillery fire, artillery guns."

Susan McClain, dispatcher at the Southport Police Department, admitted the offshore booming is spooky, but said that most folks in the area are used to it. She first heard the noise as a youngster.

"I hear it all the time," she said. "There's no pattern. It's something between a sonic boom and an earthquake."

She added, "We've had people call and say it shook windows and knocked things off the shelf. Some days it's heavier than others."

Unexplained noises similar to the "Barisal Guns" are nothing new in the field of natural phenomena. For hundreds of years, such blasts have jolted the imagination. In the early days of this country's exploration and settlement, travelers into backwoods areas frequently spoke of strange booms. The first known report of such a phenomenon in the United States was made by Lewis and Clark during an expedition near Great Falls, Montana, in 1808.

In a July journal entry, the explorers gave the following account:

"Since our arrival at the Falls we have repeatedly heard a strange noise coming from the mountains in a direction a little north of west. It is heard at different periods of the day and night, sometimes when the air is perfectly still and without a cloud, and consists of one stroke only, or five or six discharges in quick succession.

"It is loud and resembles precisely the sound of a six-pound piece of ordnance at the distance of three miles."

The mysterious sounds are called Barisal Guns for the village in India along the Ganges River where the phenomenon first came to light. Similar sounds have been heard in other parts of the world—Belgium, Italy, Japan, and Great Britain.

"Lake Guns" were once well-known phenomena in the region of Seneca Lake in New York State. In the late 1970s, *The New Scientist* magazine reported a whole series of loud booms heard along the East Coast of the United States, beginning near Charleston, South Carolina. Residents in New Jersey and as far north as Nova Scotia also reported similar noises.

Then, a few days later, Charleston was once again rocked by the mysterious blasts.

A government inquiry into the sounds was unable to offer an explanation. Most investigators concluded the noises had to have been made by aircraft, possibly supersonic military aircraft, or by artillery fire.

Some skeptics assert that the booms are made during secret Air Force tests. Roby Osborne, police chief in Long Beach, North Carolina, believes that whatever is causing the rumbling is also responsible for beach erosion.

"Ever since that started, this beach has been going," Osborne told a news agency.

Walt Workman, Osborne's assistant chief, suspects the rumblings might not be the work of nature.

"You never hear it after 6 p.m.," he said, "and I don't recall that I've ever heard it on a Sunday, but the good Lord may not want to disturb things on Sunday."

Workman said several fishermen who have heard the noise offshore insist it sounds "more like bombs being dropped on them." And, Workman went on, the booms seem "more prevalent in the summertime. Maybe it has something to do with the tides."

Theories about the continental shelf breaking off and causing the sounds should simply be discarded, according to Lanier. The slope, he said, "is very gradual in this area. The continental shelf and the slope are quite gradual and there's nothing there that could break off and make this kind of rumbling noise."

But he admits the noises are a mystery.

"We had a funny instance where they had been going off a few times, and it sounded like one morning that someone had been rolling heavy equipment over the exhibit floor room," he explained. "There was a rumbling and you could feel the building shake, just slightly, not alarming, but the way it would shake when a jet broke the sound barrier."

The only thing was, there weren't any aircraft in the area at the time.

Whether man-made or natural, the strange noises along North Carolina's coast remain one of the world's greatest unsolved mysteries.

The Philadelphia Experiment

IN THE LATE 1980s, A MOVIE was made about a U.S. ship and her crew that were mysteriously transported from one stateside port to another during a bizarre experiment involving magnetic teleportation.

Few people realized that "The Philadelphia Experiment," which went on to become a smash hit that year and remains a favorite on the videocassette market, was based on a real-life experiment conducted by the Navy during World War II.

Knowledge about the strange event first came to light in 1956 when Maurice K. Jessup, astronomer and noted researcher of unidentified flying objects, received a letter from a man identifying himself as Carlos M. Allende. Allende claimed to have witnessed the astonishing experiment that supposedly sent the *S.S. Andrew Fursenth* from its dock in Philadelphia to the Norfolk-Newport News area in a matter of seconds.

Allende also indicated that some of the crewmen aboard the ship had been lost along the way—that is, all or part of their bodies had failed to materialize upon completion of the experiment. What happened to the unfortunate crewmen was anybody's guess. Even some of those who survived went "mad as hatters," according to Allende.

Apparently the crewmen's ordeal didn't end with the experiment. In his letter, Allende indicated that months and even years after the event, men would "go blank" or occasionally fade out only to reappear elsewhere.

Sometimes these victims could be rescued by someone else holding onto their hands. This didn't always work, however. On one occasion, said Allende, a sailor began to go blank. When a friend rushed toward him and grabbed him, both began to smolder.

After reading the letter, Jessup did what any good scientific investigator would have—he went straight to the Office of Naval Research to get to the bottom of the report. The Navy promptly denied knowledge of the story and insisted it had never conducted experiments in teleportation.

Unknown to Jessup at the time, the government had also received a letter from the man purporting to be Allende. Among other things, the letter contained cryptic references to space research, UFOs, and extraterrestrial intelligence. It made rambling charges that the government was deliberately covering up its own investigation in these areas.

With the letter was sent a copy of Jessup's newest book, *The Case for the UFO,* and the bizarre story of the Philadelphia Experiment. According to Allende, Jessup had some sort of "special or secret knowledge of UFOs and life beyond the earth."

In all likelihood, Allende would have been dismissed as a crackpot and the mystery of the Philadelphia Experiment would have ended there had not a single tragic event occurred on April 29, 1959. That was when a Florida highway patrolman discovered Jessup's body slumped over his car's steering wheel in a lonely Dade County park.

The authorities ruled it a suicide. Friends of Jessup thought otherwise. Some insisted he had been murdered because he knew too much about governmental secrets—including the ill-fated Philadelphia Experiment.

Even today, more than three decades later, there are those who claim Jessup's information was correct and that he was about to go public about the Philadelphia Experiment when he died.

It seems altogether possible that research was being conducted in experimental "degaussing"—the neutralizing of magnetic fields. Breakthrough might have enabled ships (or aircraft, for that matter) to be broken up magnetically so they could pass safely over mine fields without detonation.

The ships would disappear—but only magnetically, of course. It is possible that Allende could have heard about degaussing and then allowed his imagination to take over.

Was Jessup on the verge of exposing some dark governmental secret when he died? If so, was he murdered? By whom?

There are recurring questions dealt with in books, documentaries, and lectures about UFOs and alleged government conspiracies to suppress information about the subject. The Allende letters are referred to often, as is the Air Force's abrupt decision to suspend its investigation of UFOs in 1969.

Several years after Jessup's death, a man claiming to be the real Carlos Allende stepped forward and confessed he had made the whole story up. In a speech to the Aerial Phenomena Research Organization in Tucson, Arizona, the man said he had only wanted to teach Jessup a lesson because the scientist's writings about UFOs "scared me."

Later, however, the man claiming to be Allende tried to retract his confession and was booed off the stage. Those who attended the meeting and who later met the man dismissed him as a harmless eccentric whose wild theories and rambling monologue were not to be taken seriously.

But was this man the real Carlos Allende? Or was he a government "fill in" as some investigators of the Philadelphia Experiment maintain?

Other pieces of the puzzle remain missing as well. In his original letter to Jessup, Allende said that at least one newspaper had run a story on the Philadelphia Experiment. Efforts to locate the missing story have been unsuccessful.

The Curse of 'Yellow Jack'

DURING THE 19TH CENTURY, residents of New Orleans, Mobile, Biloxi, and other Gulf Coast communities were often awakened at dawn by the surly sound of mortuary carts clattering across cobblestone squares.

As the black-draped carts made their rounds, grim-faced undertakers wearing masks and gloves would gather up corpses, sometimes piled three deep outside tightly closed doors.

"Bring out your dead...bring out your dead," became a familiar chant, especially during the long, hot summer months when evil clouds of "Yellow Jack" blew in from the sea.

Yellow Jack—or yellow fever, as the dread disease would come to be called—killed thousands of victims each year. In 1853, for example, 10,300 people died in New Orleans alone—and those from a population of only about fifty thousand.

It was so bad that on some days more than three hundred funerals were held. Relatives afraid or unwilling to bury their own deceased kinfolk would have their remains picked up by funeral carts and hauled off to common graves. Corpses piled high on top of carts would be dumped out at the cemeteries to await their turn for a grave.

"The horrors and desolations of this epidemic cannot be painted," observed one New Orleans reporter. "Neither can they be realized, except by those who have lived in New Orleans and have witnessed and participated in similar scenes. Words can convey no adequate expression...."

Entire families were wiped out by the disease, noted the reporter, "parents, children, servants, all."

Yellow Jack, one of the oldest ills known to man, had been known in the New World for a long time. The explorers and colonists who settled the swampy lowlands of Louisiana, Mississippi, and Alabama during the 17th century fell before it and learned to fear it. Oviedo, the Spanish historian, reported that a "great number" of the followers of Christopher Columbus perished from the disease in 1494.

Outbreaks of the disease resulted in numerous Caribbean expeditions being cancelled throughout the 17th and 18th centuries. More than fifty thousand of Napoleon's expeditionary force perished on the island of Santo Domingo alone.

The outbreaks were especially tragic whenever they occurred in densely populated urban areas such as New Orleans and Mobile. Until 1901, when the cause and cure of Yellow Jack were discovered, hardly a year passed without a number of communities from New Orleans to Memphis being stricken.

In the beginning, epidemics of Yellow Jack often took on supernatural connotations. Since the bodies of most victims assumed a dark and swollen look, it was often believed that demons or devils had somehow invaded the victims, consuming their vitality and draining away their souls.

Here is how one contemporary observer described bodies of victims: The corpse appears "sad, sullen, perturbed; the countenance dark, mottled, livid, swollen, and stained with blood and black vomit; the veins of the face and the whole body become distended, and look as if they were about to burst...."

Disposing of the bodies of the dead posed a problem, especially in low-lying New Orleans where the soil was so saturated with moisture content that graves deeper than three feet would fill with water. The city had traditionally built burial vaults above ground, but during epidemics, it wasn't possible to build enough, so trenches were dug and human remains sunk in the mire.

Nobody knows how many people Yellow Jack took during the early decades of Spanish rule, but in 1817, when exact records became commonplace, outbreaks were noted as annual events, always striking in summer and lasting through the early months of autumn.

In 1817, eighty cases were listed. The malady raged violently each year from 1822 until 1829 when more than a thousand persons died from the disease. The next year the mortality rate was equally high. Then came the black years of 1832 and 1833 when the city of New Orleans was stricken by both yellow fever and Asiatic cholera.

In 1833, ten thousand persons were known to have died from yellow fever alone. As always, that figure was probably low, given the fact that not everybody reported the illness.

Yellow Jack was an excruciatingly painful disease that attacked the blood and liver, then spread quickly to the digestive tract, kidneys, and brain. This gave the skin a jaundiced color and the illness a name.

But the chief symptom was a black vomit, called "el vomito negro" by the Spaniards. The painful vomiting usually lasted seven days, by the end of which the patient had either recovered or died.

No one knew what caused the disease. There were a lot of theories, most of them associated with decaying wood, stagnant pools of water, and offshore winds that some people believed blew in the disease.

"Yellow Fever houses"—places where victims had died— were destroyed along with all furnishings and clothing to prevent the disease from spreading.

Not until 1901 did authorities make a breakthrough. That year, U.S. army doctors determined that female mosquitoes of a certain species, *Stegomyia calopus,* transmitted the highly contagious disease. Prevention suddenly was easy. Stagnant water was covered with chemical solutions that destroyed the unhatched larvae of the female mosquito. Sulphur could be sprayed into the air to fumigate those in flight.

Though scattered outbreaks would continue, no longer did residents of the Gulf Coast states have to fear Yellow Jack the way they once did. The surly sound of the funeral cart was a relic of the past.

California's Fallen Angel

ON MAY 18, 1926, A PRETTY young woman vacationing alone at a seaside hotel near Venice, California, slipped into a striking green swimsuit and strolled to the beach for a quick splash in the surf.

When she failed to check back in at the desk a few hours later, hotel authorities began to worry. Soon a police patrol was combing the beach for signs of the missing guest. Lifeguards paddled out beyond the breakers, divers scoured the sea floor, and airplanes swooped low over the waves.

By nightfall, hundreds of frantic people had gathered along the shore to pray for the young woman. They sobbed, sang hymns, and chanted. One girl committed suicide on the spot. Minutes later, a young man jumped into the dark sea shouting, "I'm going after her," and drowned.

Every day for the next month and a half, the search of the beach continued. Some held out hope she would return to them alive, and so kept bonfires roaring on the windy beach at night. Newspaper reporters hounded the hotel. A twenty-five thousand dollar reward was offered to anyone who found the body.

Why was so much fuss being made over one lady tourist?

This was no ordinary lady. Her name was Aimee Semple McPherson—"Sister Aimee" to her millions of faithful followers around the world. Sister Aimee, a beautiful, vivacious, once-widowed, once-divorced woman of thirty-six, was one of the most famous people in the world. She was the charismatic founder and spiritual leader of the Angelus Temple, a

Los Angeles-based religious cult that sponsored revivalist meetings throughout the United States and in several foreign countries. She rubbed elbows with the movers and shakers of the day—movie stars, athletes, politicians, even the president of the United States.

In the early 1920s, her Temple was a gathering place for thousands of people seeking salvation. Eventually the colossal structure boasted an auditorium capable of seating five thousand, a vast collection of Hollywood-style costumes for Aimee and her choir, and a "miracle room" piled high with hundreds of discarded crutches, trusses, and wheelchairs.

At services, Aimee entertained visitors with dazzling pageants, lantern slides, music, dramatized sermons, shows, circuses, and healing sessions. According to one writer who monitored the activities of the Temple, Sister Aimee "invited the folks to feel at home, to relax, to have a good time. She released their minds from frightful visions of eternal damnation. Instead she gave them flowers, music, golden trumpets, red robes, angels, incense, nonsense, and sex appeal...."

Aimee's rise to the top of the evangelical world had been meteoric. Only five years earlier, she had arrived in Los Angeles with less than a hundred dollars in her pocket and driving a dilapidated automobile. A complete unknown, she drew upon her uncanny ability to manipulate people and quickly amassed a fortune by collecting money from her semihysterical adherents with an ease that was the envy of many conventional church ministers.

By 1926, Sister Aimee was one of the richest, most popular, most beloved women in the world. When she disappeared on the beach that bright day in May, it was for many as if a light had gone out in the world.

Her passing was mourned by millions. Special services were held from California to China. A thirty-six thousand dollar memorial was quickly built in her honor, financed by the generous donations of her churchgoers. It was the least they could do for their angelic healer of the sick and lame, their guiding light for the lost.

Then, shortly after midnight on June 23, a strange thing happened. A bedraggled woman claiming to be the famous evangelist staggered to a house near the Mexican border town of Agua Prieta and demanded to use a telephone. When police arrived a few minutes later she told them she was none other than Sister Aimee and that she had escaped the day before from a gang of kidnappers hiding in the desert.

It was a miracle! God had heard the prayers of Sister Aimee's multitude and had clearly sent her back to resume her good work. At the Temple, bells chimed and the sanctuary echoed with hymns and shouts of hallelujah.

Newspapers, of course, had a field day with the evangelist's miraculous reappearance. Day after day, headlines told and retold how Sister Aimee had been lured into a car by abductors who apparently had planned to kidnap other famous people in a bizarre billion-dollar ransom scheme.

It all sounded fine until information finally surfaced that Sister Aimee's radio operator, Kenneth G. Ormiston, had also disappeared on the same day she claimed to have been abducted. Soon rumors were flying that the adored evangelist had been having a secret affair with her married radioman and that the kidnapping story was nothing more than a hoax.

Sister Aimee demanded official vindication. She urged the police to track down the kidnappers and requested that an investigative grand jury be convened immediately.

At her hearing, the district attorney dutifully noted that it would have been virtually impossible to walk across the Mexican desert, as Sister Aimee claimed to have done, from noon to midnight without water. In the end, no evidence was found to indict anyone for kidnapping, and the sweet-talking preacher's story was discredited.

The worst was yet to come.

Shortly after the jury disbanded, four credible witnesses stepped forward to say Sister Aimee matched the description of a woman who had occupied a bungalow in Carmel with Ormiston during the month of May. Pieces of Aimee's sermons were found in the house along with a grocery slip in her handwriting.

In September, a criminal complaint was filed charging Aimee and others with a conspiracy to obstruct justice. The preliminary hearing lasted nearly two months, during which time Sister Aimee charged that religious rivals were behind a nefarious attempt to have her defrocked as the leading revivalist of the day.

On October 28, a newspaper published some love letters it had discovered; they were apparently written to Ormiston in Aimee's own handwriting. Ormiston himself was later tracked down in Pennsylvania, but on January 4, 1927, District Attorney Asa Keyes suddenly moved to dismiss the case.

Why? Rumor had it that the district attorney—who was jailed a few weeks later for corrupt conduct—had accepted a thirty thousand dollar bribe from the Temple.

Whatever happened, the damage had already been done. A series of bad business investments left Sister Aimee strapped for cash. Then, a few weeks after the trial ended, the crowds stopped coming to the Temple. The cavernous auditorium which once rocked with the sound of thousands of voices now stood empty and quiet. Gone were the pageants, the red-robed choir, and the glitzy sermons.

Over the next two decades, Aimee was sued in Los Angeles courts fifty-five times for unpaid bills, broken contracts, overdue promissory notes, malicious prosecution, and slander. On the morning of September 27, 1944, Sister Aimee was found unconscious in a hotel in Oakland, California. The night before she had given her final sermon before ten thousand wary listeners.

In her handbag was a bottle containing twenty sleeping pills. Several other unidentified capsules were found scattered on the floor.

She died later that same day. The coroner's report attributed her death to "shock and respiratory failure due to an overdose of barbital compound and a kidney ailment."

Two days later, a small crowd clad in robes and clutching hymnals gathered one last time inside the Angelus Temple to bid their mysterious and maligned founder a fond farewell.

Into the Unknown

Judge Crater's Ride into the Unknown

JOSEPH FORCE CRATER LIVED the kind of life most men can only dream of. Young, handsome, and rich, the successful forty-one-year-old New York lawyer enjoyed the pleasures the world had to offer—yachts, travel, fast cars, private retreats, and beautiful women.

As president of the prestigious Democratic Party Club of Manhattan, he was also very powerful—so powerful, in fact, that in April of 1930 he was appointed to the New York State Supreme Court.

In those days, Judge Crater was probably the most popular man in New York City. Ambitious, hard-working, and gifted with persuasive charm, he possessed an uncanny knack for being in the right place at the right time. He quickly became the darling of the New York media; hardly a day went by without his picture appearing in the newspaper or his name being mentioned on the radio.

A bright political career obviously lay before this tall, dapper ladies' man who parted his iron-gray hair neatly down the middle. All he had to do was stay out of trouble—and remember who his friends were down at Tammany Hall.

On the evening of August 6, 1930, less than four months after his appointment to the bench, Judge Crater disappeared. One minute he had been laughing and talking with friends outside a Manhattan restaurant, the next, he waved goodbye, stepped into a cab, and was never seen or heard from again.

Crater's ride into the unknown prompted one of the most massive manhunts in New York history. After years of investigation costing millions of dollars and covering several states, the fate of Joseph Force Crater remains an unsolved mystery.

After all this time, it is still a puzzle how—and why—a man of Judge Crater's reputation and stature could suddenly vanish from the face of the earth without a trace.

To get a grip on the facts, it helps to go back to that summer in 1930 when Crater and his family were vacationing at their cottage in Belgrade Lakes, Maine. On August 3, he told his wife, Stella, that he had to go back to New York for a few days, but he didn't explain why.

Three days later, on the morning of August 6, he spent several hours at his courthouse chamber desk going through some old files. That afternoon he instructed his assistant, Joseph Mara, to cash two checks for him in the amount of $5,150. When Mara returned with the money, he helped the judge carry two locked briefcases to his Fifth Avenue apartment, and then was told he could take the rest of the day off.

That same evening, Crater met two friends—a lawyer and a showgirl—at a restaurant on West 45th Street and joined them for dinner. Nothing unusual happened that night, according to the lawyer's testimony, and at exactly 9:10 p.m., Crater, dressed in a double-breasted brown suit, gray spats, and a high collar, waved goodbye to his companions and stepped into a taxi.

That was the last anybody ever saw of Judge Crater.

Ironically, nothing happened for almost two weeks. One of the most prominent and powerful men in America had disappeared, and nobody even noticed.

It wasn't until ten days later, August 16, that Mrs. Crater called up the courthouse to inquire about her husband's whereabouts. A secretary told her everything was all right, not to worry, that the missing judge was probably off tending to political business and would eventually show up.

By August 25, the day court sessions began, Crater still hadn't returned. Alarmed, his fellow justices had launched a private search, managing somehow to keep the affair out of the newspaper. Nothing turned up, however, and on August 26, the disappearance became front page news.

A police investigation revealed that the judge's bank deposit box was empty, as was a private safe, and two personal briefcases were missing. Foul play was immediately suspected, though rumors were flying around town that the judge had simply skipped out, perhaps with a girlfriend he had reportedly been seen with in recent months.

A grand jury was quickly convened to get to the bottom of the case. After ninety-five witnesses had testified and nine hundred seventy-five pages of testimony had been amassed, the foreman concluded in a written statement: "The evidence is insufficient to warrant any expression of opinion as to whether Crater is alive or dead, or as to whether he has absented himself voluntarily, or is a sufferer from disease in the nature of amnesia, or is the victim of a crime."

In other words, Judge Crater had simply vanished, and it would be fruitless to continue the investigation.

Mrs. Crater, who had fallen in love with and married Crater in 1916 after he had successfully represented her in a divorce settlement, thought otherwise. She and a close group of friends continued to search for clues on their own, convinced that foul play was behind her husband's mysterious disappearance.

Mrs. Crater went on record several times as saying her husband had been murdered "because of a sinister something that was connected with politics." She even had a suspect—Tammany Hall itself. It was her opinion that "forces" within that organization had killed Judge Crater because he refused to pay them back for helping with his nomination to the bench.

Other theories linked the judge's fate to organized crime. In his judicial role, Crater had once helped put together a lucrative deal involving the sale of a Manhattan hotel. Some investigators suggested that the transaction went sour for a certain group of people who saw revenge as the only way to vindicate their losses.

The most likely explanation, according to Emil K. Ellis, another New York attorney, was that Crater had been murdered in a showgirl's blackmail scheme. Ellis, who represented Crater's widow in a lawsuit against her husband's insurance company, said the $5,150 in cash the judge had withdrawn the day before he disappeared was probably a payoff. Crater was then killed by a gangster friend of the showgirl when he refused to give her more money.

On June 6, 1939, almost nine years to the day after he went missing, Judge Crater was declared legally dead. The case was never officially closed, and reports about his reappearance continue to pop up more than sixty years later.

Amelia Earhart's Last Flight

A FEW DAYS BEFORE Christmas in 1936, an American airliner carrying fifty passengers disappeared on a flight between Salt Lake City and Los Angeles. For the next few weeks, teams of rescue workers combed the rugged hills and desolate terrain in an unsuccessful attempt to locate the missing plane and any possible survivors.

The investigators were about to give up when they received a startling phone call. On the other end of the line was Amelia Earhart, the famous female flyer who had made aviation history only a few years before with her solo Atlantic Ocean crossing. Speaking as if in a daze, Amelia told them exactly what had happened to the doomed aircraft and where to look for it.

"The plane is down in the Wasatch Mountains," she said, her voice crackling on the other end of the line. "The passengers and pilots are dead. Their bodies have been robbed by a trapper."

The eerie revelation would have been dismissed as a crank call had it not been for Amelia Earhart's reputation. She was not only a hero and pioneer in the infant field of aviation, she was also an international celebrity, wife of an equally famous book publisher and film magnate, George Putnam.

Acting on the tip, rescue authorities rushed into the mountains and found the wreckage exactly where Earhart had said it would be. The passengers and crew, all dead, had been stripped of money and valuables. Some months later, a trapper reportedly appeared in a Salt Lake City bar and, after a few tongue-loosening drinks, announced to the bartender his discovery of the crashed airliner.

Before authorities could question him, however, the trapper escaped back into the mountains and was never heard from again.

Just how had Amelia Earhart known about the downed airliner and the grisly events that followed with the trapper? That's a question that has bothered investigators ever since—especially in light of the well-publicized fact that Earhart claimed to possess psychic powers linking her with the spirit world.

By the mid-1930s, it was no secret that the lanky, tousle-haired flyer attended séances and frequently consulted mediums. In newspaper and radio interviews she told about having her own special "contact" in the world beyond who occasionally tuned her in to future events.

In demonstration of her gifts, Earhart often made other startling predictions. On another occasion, she accurately revealed the whereabouts of a missing airliner that had crashed in the California hills north of Burbank.

Her uncanny ability to "see" airplane crashes before they happened and then to guide rescuers to their location would continue to astonish a generation of Americans.

In light of her startling predictions, some biographers and followers became convinced that Earhart indeed possessed genuine psychic powers. There are those who have also wondered whether or not she had even received some kind of spiritual warning about her own doomed flight in 1937.

On July 1, 1937, only a few months after she had shaken the world with her startling psychic revelations involving the downed airliners, Amelia Earhart climbed aboard her twin-engine Lockheed Elektra for what was to be the last leg of her headline-making flight around the world. With her was Fred Noonan, a tall Irishman who was her navigator.

From Lae, New Guinea, the flight was to take the pair to Howland, a tiny Pacific atoll 2,570 miles away. There they were to establish radio contact with a U.S. Coast Guard ship that would guide them the rest of the way on their global journey, which they would break up in a series of short, leisurely hops.

Early the next morning, July 2, the Coast Guard ship received the following message from Earhart: "Gas is running low." An hour later, she gave a final location report, and then disappeared. Neither she nor Noonan were seen or heard from again.

It was assumed that their plane had simply run out of fuel and crashed into the ocean. Almost immediately, squadrons of airplanes and fleets of ships were dispatched to the area in an attempt to locate the downed Elektra. At the time, it was the largest air-sea search that had ever been formed.

At the special request of President Roosevelt, the U.S. Navy sent the carrier *Lexington*, the battleship *Colorado*, and a dozen other vessels. Ships and planes reportedly scoured some 262,000 square miles of the Pacific.

After days of combing the ocean and hundreds of small islands in the area, the hunt was called off. In its official report, the Navy declared that Noonan and Earhart were "lost at sea," and closed the book on the case.

There were others, however, who didn't want to give up. There were some, in fact, who believed strongly that there was more to the case than was first apparent.

For years, some of Earhart's fans claimed to have uncovered proof that the forty-year-old aviator had been commissioned by the United States government to spy on Japanese facilities in the Pacific area. Some of those who subscribe to this theory claim she was captured by the Japanese when her plane went down and later was executed as a spy.

In the 1960s, a newspaper reporter interested in the case heard about a Saipanese woman who once claimed to have seen two American flyers—a man and a woman—on Saipan Island in the Marianas in 1937 when the islands were under

Japanese occupation. Her descriptions of the flyers matched Earhart and Noonan, down to hair color and height.

The reporter, Fred Goerner, flew to Saipan and interviewed several more people who said they had seen the missing Americans. One man even took him to an unmarked grave where he said a white man and woman were buried. The couple had "come down from the sky a long time ago," the man explained.

In concluding his investigation, Goerner quoted a high-ranking American official who stated that Amelia Earhart "had some sort of understanding with officials of the government that the last part of her flight around the world would be over those Japanese islands."

To this day, the fate of Amelia Earhart and her Irish navigator remains an international puzzle.

The Elusive Bridey Murphy

"TONIGHT I WILL ATTEMPT an experiment in hypnosis that I have never before undertaken. The subject will be Ruth Simmons."

With these words, spoken into a crackling tape recorder one night in November of 1952, began one of the most intriguing investigations into the paranormal ever made. Although he couldn't know it at the time, the middle-aged amateur hypnotist in charge of the experiment was about to make history—and send shock waves through psychic research circles that would last a decade.

The man was Morey Bernstein, and he was a successful Colorado businessman. Before him, stretched out on a sofa sound asleep, lay Ruth Simmons, a young housewife from Denver. Together, they were about to embark on a journey that would lead them to a place it was thought no mortal could go—the past.

For most of his adult life, Bernstein had believed in reincarnation, a mystical doctrine shared by millions of Buddhists and Hindus around the world. Central to the belief is the view that souls do not die, and until they achieve sufficient enlightenment, they keep being reborn into new bodies upon the death of the old.

Bernstein was no wild-eyed kook. A graduate of the University of Pennsylvania's prestigious Wharton School of Finance, he was the hard-working sales director of his family's prosperous hardware and farm implements firm in Pueblo, Colorado. A serious man, he read nothing but novels and business magazines; according to his wife, Hazel, he "knew of and cared nothing for occult stuff."

But reincarnation was different. So was hypnosis. At the time, a lot of entertainers and respected scientists were publicly professing their belief in the theory. They were in pretty good company, too—Schopenhauer, Emerson, Whitman, Goethe, Pythagoras, and Plato were among the many celebrated intellects who over the centuries also accepted reincarnation as fact.

Some years earlier, Bernstein had discovered his own amazing powers of hypnosis, and this seemed to have awakened within the tough Westerner a dormant interest in the powers of the mind in general. He began to read everything on the subject he could get his hands on, especially the works of Edgar Cayce, America's "sleeping prophet," because of his stunning abilities to predict the future, diagnose illnesses, and travel into the past or the future through self-induced states of hypnosis.

Bernstein was especially drawn to an experimental new form of hypnosis called "age regression." He honestly believed that if a person could be taken back in a trance state to the period of his earliest infancy, there was nothing to prevent the hypnotist from taking him back to the womb—perhaps to whatever lay beyond.

All he needed was a willing and compliant subject.

One night at a party, he and Hazel happened to meet a particularly bright and vivacious young brunette who has been called "Ruth Simmons." (Her real identity was not revealed until years later, to protect her from adverse publicity and because of the unique circumstances involved in the experiment.) Fascinated by the idea of age regression, "Ruth" begged Bernstein "to put her under." He agreed.

On Saturday, November 29, 1952, Ruth arrived at Bernstein's Pueblo home to begin the session. At precisely 10:30 p.m., Morey Bernstein switched his tape recorder on, leaned over Ruth's relaxed form on the sofa, and began to count to ten as he waved a burning candle slowly a few inches from Ruth's face. Within seconds, her breathing became deep and regular.

"We are going to turn back through time and space, just like turning the pages of a book," Bernstein droned soothingly to her. "And when I next talk to you…when I next talk to you…you will be seven years old."

Bernstein was pleased; the procedure couldn't be going any better. With the sound of the tape recorded whirring in the background, Ruth Simmons suddenly began to talk—softly at first, hesitantly, as if she weren't quite sure where she was. On Bernstein's gentle instructions, she began to relax.

Then her voice began to change. In high, youthful tones, she began quickly to recount details of her childhood—first high school, then grade school, all the way back to kindergarten, her voice growing progressively more childlike every step of the way. Further and further she slipped back, her words becoming garbled, infantile.

When she was one year old, Bernstein ordered her to stop going back. He glanced up a Ruth's husband, Rex, crouching on the other side of the sofa. He smiled, a signal that he was about to continue—to go where no other hypnotist had ever gone.

"Back, back, and back…until oddly enough you find yourself in some other scene, some other place, some other time, and when I talk to you again you will tell us about it."

The room fell silent. Outside, the November wind howled around the modest frame house, driving spears of rain against the draped and shuttered windows. The clock on the mantel above the sofa where Ruth Simmons lay struck eleven.

The next few moments were among the most exciting in the history of parapsychology. Books would be written about the strange events soon to take place in the Bernstein household. Movies and television films would recreate the episode for generations of disbelieving Americans. Even Bernstein's own book about his work would become a best seller, making him a very wealthy man.

From beyond the grave it came: a soft, sad, little girl's voice that spoke in an unfamiliar accent and seemed agitated for having been disturbed.

"...scratched the paint off all my bed!"

Bernstein gasped. Swallowing hard, he pressed on with his interview, asking the only logical question he could think of under the circumstances.

"Why did you do that?"

The new voice told how she had been spanked and sent to bed for some childish offense and had scratched at the paint on her bed for revenge against her parents.

"What is your name?" Bernstein asked.

In that same childlike voice, Ruth Simmons replied, "Friday...Friday Murphy."

As the investigation later revealed, the name was actually Bridey Murphy, and she lived in the county of Cork, Ireland, with her father, a lawyer named Duncan, and her mother, Kathleen. They lived in a white wooden house. The year was 1806, and Bridey Murphy said she was eight years old.

Throughout the long night Bernstein continued to ask the phantom girl questions—what she ate for breakfast, the names of her dolls, the names of her brothers and sisters, where she went to school and church. "Bridey" always answered each question—even blushing when she said the color of her hair was red.

Later, as Bernstein fast-forwarded into the young Irish girl's future, he learned that she had married a Belfast lawyer named Brian McCarthy, a Catholic, although she herself was a Protestant. They attended a church in the north called St. Theresa's where the priest's name was Father John. They had no children.

At last came the most dramatic moment of the evening— Bridey Murphy McCarthy's death at the age of sixty-six after falling down a steep flight of stairs in her home.

"Can you tell us what happened after your death?" Bernstein persisted. "Can you tell us what happened after you died?"

"I didn't do...like Father John said. I didn't go to pur-gatory. I stayed right in that house until Father John died. Oh, he died...I saw him. I saw him when he died."

"And then you talked to him?"

"Yes."

Bernstein couldn't repress a shudder; *it was like interviewing a ghost!*

The ghost told him how she had seen her husband die, too, and then had wandered about "feeling neither emotion nor desire...for a long time...until...I was reborn as Ruth Mills."

There the session ended. Over the next eleven months, Bernstein would conduct six more trance interviews with the voice of Bridey Murphy. In his book *The Search for Bridey Murphy*, the author reveled hundreds of tiny details that were added to the first basic outline of her life and death.

The next couple of years were busy ones for Bernstein, who sought to prove the reality of reincarnation through his taped interviews and writings about Bridey Murphy. Keeping an agreement with his publisher, the author traveled to Ireland to research Bridey's "real life." Lawyers were hired, as well as various librarians, to help track down old records.

Some facts dug up from the dusty files tended to support Bernstein's contention that he had, in fact, communicated with a woman who had lived in Ireland over a century ago. Names, churches, shops, and villages all seemed to correspond to actual people and places. Even Bridey's dialect checked out.

The bubble burst, however, when a newspaper reporter found out the elusive Mrs. Simmons—who had shown little interest in all the publicity—had been raised by an aunt of Irish extraction. Surely, charged the editorials, that explained the "mystery" of Bridey Murphy. Tales from her distant childhood of Irish history and customs, had undoubtedly lodged themselves in Ruth Simmons's subconscious and re-emerged under hypnosis.

To further weaken her story, no official record was ever found of the house she claimed to have lived in, nor did the birth and death of herself or her husband show up.

But some of the details did tally. For instance, her journey from Belfast to Cork was described as only one who had made it could have done. Also, her accounts of shopping for provisions at a grocery store named "Farr" appear true, because such a shop actually existed where and when she said it did.

Was it a hoax? Did Morey Bernstein and "Ruth Simmons" concoct the entire scheme, perhaps for the fame and fortune that followed?

For years, psychiatrists and psychologists studying the case wavered on making a determination. Those familiar with hypnosis contended it was possible that highly suggestible subjects were likely to react on the slightest hint offered by the hypnotist. It was demonstrated that, on occasion, some subjects under hypnosis can speak in a foreign language not used since childhood and can suddenly remember long-forgotten details about earlier years of their lives.

Two decades after her first hypnotic session with Morey Bernstein, Ruth Simmons—whose real name was "Mrs. Morrow"—was asked if she had ever tried to recapture Bridey Murphy again.

"It has been twenty years since I was Bridey Murphy. I have never done anything like it again and I never will."

St. Brendan's Voyage

WHO GOT HERE FIRST? Every American schoolchild knows that Christopher Columbus discovered America in the year 1492 when he "sailed the ocean blue" and landed on the tiny island of Guanahana, which he promptly renamed San Salvador (Holy Savior).

But was he *really* the first person to step foot in the New World?

Of course not.

Archaeologists tell us that tens of thousands of years ago—perhaps as many as seventy-five-thousand—wandering bands of nomads crossed a now-submerged landbridge connecting Asia with Alaska. Long before the arrival of Columbus, these Asiatic hunters had settled the far corners of the New World, from the frozen reaches of northern Canada to the tip of South America.

Even if we give the Genoan mariner credit for being the first to bring news of the New World to Europe, it is likely that other Europeans came before him. Romans, Etruscans, Phoenicians, Welshmen, Scandinavians, and even Irishmen are among ancient and medieval voyagers frequently mentioned in early legends and sagas as having explored or settled portions of what might correctly be called pre-Columbian America.

In fact, historians and archaeologists such as Barry Fell of California and Joseph Mahan of Georgia now assert that the Atlantic Ocean might have been a veritable freeway linking the old and new worlds in ancient and medieval times.

Mahan, for example, thinks he has found evidence suggesting that ancient Hebrews reached the hills of Tennessee in the first century A.D. Mahan bases his claim on a rock tablet found in Loudon County in 1889. Inscriptions on the tablet, unearthed along with nine human skeletons from a single mound, were translated to read "A Comet for the Jews"—an obvious reference to one of the skeletons who had been the group's "comet," or leader, according to Cyrus Gordon, a Semitic languages expert who worked with Mahan on deciphering the tablet.

Barry Fell—now retired from Harvard University—has long argued his theory that North America was explored and settled thousands of years ago by various groups of Europeans and Africans. In his book *America B.C.,* Fell points to hundreds of stone tablets, graves, and other bits of evidence in North America, linking them with transatlantic voyagers.

Experts such as Fell and Mahan believe luck and skilled seamanship probably accounted for many such long voyages by ancient mariners. Plagues, droughts, and invasions by enemies might have contributed to motivating the journeys, these scholars maintain.

Centuries-old Viking sagas tell how Leif Ericson and other Norsemen sailed beyond Greenland to "Vinland," or "Vineland," which some historians believed was located along the North American coast. Since the record of Ericson's voyages was mixed with legendary stories, however, the entire notion was dismissed as fable.

Then, in the 1960s, the first solid evidence emerged from the frozen ground of Newfoundland that indicated there might be something to the old stories after all. Norwegian explorer Helge Instad and his archaeologist wife Anne Stine uncovered numerous artifacts—as well as what appeared to be the remains of a Viking settlement. Subsequent excavation confirmed their theory that Viking voyagers had settled Greenland more than a thousand years ago.

Shortly after the Vikings came Welshmen, led by their legendary leader, Prince Madoc. Some historians believe Madoc sailed into Mobile Bay, set up camp, then pressed northward into Alabama, where he befriended Indians and established colonies. Some of his men allegedly intermarried with the locals, giving rise to legends of blue-eyed Indians.

But of all the fanciful tales of discovery, none rivals that of St. Brendan, an Irish monk, and his fabled seven-year voyage to the "promised land of the saints." Although some scholars see it as nothing more than an outstanding religious allegory, others believe the hearty band of Celtic monks were the vanguard of Irish sailors who explored the new World long before other Europeans.

Setting out from Ireland in their thirty-six foot hide-covered boat called a "curragh," St. Brendan and his companions discovered many fascinating worlds—including an island where the sheep were white as snow, another where the birds chanted prayers with them, and another covered with fire and ice. They even were supposed to have celebrated Easter while aground on the back of a giant sea serpent or whale. A few days later, they sailed through "coagulated waters" before entering another sea so clear they could see the fish curled up on the bottom like cats.

Modern researchers say the island of fire and ice might have been volcanic Iceland with its surrounding icebergs. The clear sea, they say, could have been the sparkling Bahamas, and the "coagulated waters" could have been none other than the weed-choked Sargasso Sea.

During the seventeenth and eighteenth centuries, Spanish and Portuguese explorers in Florida believed they had found evidence that St. Brendan's expedition had reached the shores of the St. John's River near St. Augustine.

As incredible as it seems, some modern scholars think there might have been a grain of truth behind St. Brendan's voyage to the "promised land," or "The Fortunate Isles," as the destination was referred to in other accounts. It is known that Viking raiders were swarming over Ireland during the time of St. Brendan, and that many monks fled for their lives—often by sea.

It is also known that these monks—who were the finest Christian scholars west of Byzantium—had knowledge of island refuges far to the west. They also possessed advanced maritime skills, having often sailed to the Shetlands and Faroes and finally to Iceland—perhaps even to Greenland. From there, a voyage to North America was a relatively easy hop.

In 1977, a British sailor named Timothy Severin set out to prove that monks during Brendan's time had the skill and technology to make such a long voyage. Severin built a curragh similar to Brendan's and successfully completed the 2,600-mile journey from Ireland to Newfoundland.

In the Realm of Spirits

Graveyards and Ghostly Lights

THE FIRST TIME BILL MACK saw the eerie blue light twinkling outside his camper window, he wasn't surprised.

In fact, the California author and fisherman had been expecting the strange light to appear. He had heard stories, weird stories about a mysterious ball of light that haunted the lonely coastal wilds of southern California and the Baja California peninsula.

The local Mexicans called it the *"luz peculiar"*—or "strange light." For centuries, Indians living along the Gulf of California had known the phenomenon as the "great sea spirit," a capricious demigod that occasionally blew ashore from its distant watery world beyond the horizon.

Bill Mack knew all that, and he also knew that no one had ever been hurt by the light—so far, anyway. Still, he wasn't in a mood to take chances, so when he was awakened that sultry night by the eerie glow at his window, his first instinct was to crank up the camper and flee those gloomy woods beside the crashing sea.

He held his ground. He had come too far to let the infamous spooklight of southern California chase him away.

Armed only with his trusty little Yashica-Mat, the experienced photojournalist was determined to face whatever terror came his way—natural or supernatural—and capture on film one of the West Coast's greatest unsolved mysteries.

"It appeared to be about fifty yards long," Mack said about the light in a national magazine article, "and I estimated its phosphorescence extended about twenty-five feet in the air. There it sat, just a blob of blue light."

Even though the details of his ghostly encounter were read by thousands, the few pictures he got were unfortunately "of extremely poor quality….[T]he light showed as a tiny glow in the center of…intense black."

And so another chapter was written on one of America's least understood phenomena: spooklights. Those amazing little tentacles of fire have reportedly been seen over the years by millions of people from California to Connecticut. No other phenomenon has so bewildered, so frightened, and so entertained generations of Americans as has this vexing apparition, whose place in natural history as well as folklore has long been firmly established.

In spite of all the sightings, little is known about spooklights. They appear to be largely indigenous to the North American continent—although unconfirmed reports have been made in the Soviet Union and China. And they generally share a similar form, usually manifested as a bobbing or hovering blue light.

They haunt some of the loneliest places imaginable—swamps, forests, bogs, mountains, seashores, and graveyards—but they frequently are seen dancing and bobbing along railroad tracks, highways, and even city streets. Quite a few spooklights seem to prefer customary locations, often returning night after night at the same time to put on a show for anyone brave enough to stick around and observe.

For centuries, beginning with the Indians, "experts" have sought to understand what causes a spooklight. Despite countless field investigations such as those conducted by Bill Mack and others, nobody seems any closer to an answer than were the Cherokees who believed they were simply wandering spirits. Many theories have been advanced to account for their bizarre existence, but so far nothing seems to satisfy the majority of investigators. Explanations range from the scientific to the supernatural—and, as one might suspect in such matters, it's usually the supernaturalists who triumph in any serious debate or inquiry.

One of the most popular tales of a spooklight haunting comes from the Colorado high country "ghost town" of Silver Cliff. Back in the 1880s, Silver Cliff was a boom town, inhabited by five thousand rip-roaring miners. It was then that the strange light was first spotted, weaving over a local cemetery.

Over the years, however, the phenomenon became a regular feature at the old graveyard, often making appearances for scientists, journalists, and others who came to observe its capricious antics.

In 1956, a local newspaper conducted the first serious investigation of the phenomenon. A decade later, on August 20, 1967, the *New York Times* ran a story on the Silver Cliff lights. Two years after that, *National Geographic* sent its assistant editor, Edward J. Linehan, to personally look into the mystery and deliver a story.

Linehan's account is now considered one of the most accurate, enthralling accounts of a spooklight investigation on record. On his first night out, he saw them—"dim, round spots of blue-white light" glowing over several rows of cracked and crumbling tombstones.

For the next fifteen minutes, Linehan, accompanied by a local resident, pursued the elusive lights among the lonely graves. Bill Kleine, the local who escorted the editor on his strange mission, disputed theories that the lights were caused by reflections of town lights in the distance. "My wife and I have both seen these lights when the fog was so thick that you couldn't see [the town] at all."

There are literally thousands of such spooklights all over North America, some more famous and well-documented than either the Silver Cliff or Gulf of California cases. Along the New England coast, for example, people have known the "Palatine Light" for more than two centuries. In Missouri, there is even a town named in honor of some of its glowing residents—Spooksville.

L. W. Robertson, curator of the Spooksville Museum, admits to having an open mind on the subject, even though he's aware that the ghost lights are responsible for the town's number one industry, tourism. "I have no idea what the spooklight is, and I've looked at it as much as any living man," he is on record as saying.

It was during World War II, in fact, that Robertson first heard about spooklights. That's when he accompanied the U.S. Army Corps of Engineers on an expedition in and around the county in an effort to unravel the timeless riddle.

After checking local caves, testing mineral deposits, and conducting aerial surveys of roadways and the surrounding countryside for miles, the Corps's investigation for the Army High Command was inconclusive.

Perhaps there is no rational explanation for the enigmatic lights that haunt so much of the American countryside. And perhaps that's just as well.

Edward Linehan, in his concluding remarks in the *National Geographic* article, expressed it best when he said this: "No doubt someone, someday, will prove there's nothing at all supernatural in the luminous manifestations of Silver Cliff's cemetery. And I will feel a tinge of disappointment. I prefer to believe they are the restless stirrings of the ghosts of Colorado, eager to get their Centennial State on with its pressing business; seeking out and working the bonanzas of a second glorious century,"

The Possession of Mary Lurancy Vennum

ONE WINTER NIGHT IN 1878, a tall, distinguished-looking gentleman carrying a small black bag climbed down from his horse-drawn carriage before a handsome, elegantly appointed house in the small town of Milford in eastern Illinois. He was quickly ushered in.

A sense of urgency filled the spacious, well-lit home as he was rushed up a winding flight of stairs to a bedroom at the far end of the hall. From beyond the bedroom door came an eerie mixture of sounds—the unmistakable laughter of a child interspersed by wild, animalistic grunts.

"This way, please," the gaunt, teary-eyed host said, leading the way into the room.

Dr. E. W. Stevens took a deep breath, and followed by the host and a friend of the family, named Roff, stepped across the threshold. As a doctor and researcher, Stevens had encountered many strange cases, but all his years of medicine hadn't prepared him for the sight that awaited him in the flickering shadows of the dreary Victorian-style bedroom.

On the high four-poster bed crouched a pretty young girl, about thirteen, clad in a long, ruffled nightgown, with black hair cascading around her narrow shoulders. It seemed the girl was in pain; her dark eyes rolled back in the head while she made strange, hissing sounds through clenched teeth. What unnerved the doctor most was the girl's attitude of composure.

"She's been like this for weeks," the girl's father explained sadly.

Stevens studied the situation for a moment, then sat down next to the girl. He gently took her hand, and after some difficulty, managed to quiet the young patient.

"Tell me what's troubling you, my child," the doctor said softly. "I can help you."

For the next several minutes, Stevens listened patiently as Mary Lurancy Vennum recounted her incredible story. In a clear, steady voice she told him how for the past three years or so, ghosts had visited her room on a regular basis—first in her dreams, then more and more often while she was awake.

"Ghosts? What kind of ghosts?" the doctor asked, intrigued.

"They weren't just ghosts," Mary Lurancy replied. "I saw heaven and angels and a lot of other ghosts who talked to me just as you are talking to me now."

The girl went on to explain that many of the "ghosts" who came to her were people she had known in life—aunts, uncles, and other deceased relatives. The ghost that frightened her most was that of a young woman named Mary Roff who wanted to control her.

"Mary Roff!" Mr. Roff exclaimed, rushing quickly toward the bed. "That is my daughter. Why, she has been in heaven for twelve years!"

Roff told how his daughter had died in July, 1865, at the age of eighteen, having been tormented by epileptic seizures throughout most of her life. Roff, who previously hadn't believed in ghosts, wondered whether it could be possible that his late daughter was returning from the grave to take over Mary Lurancy's body.

Indeed, Mary Lurancy was giving every sign of being Mary Roff and was constantly pleading to be allowed to go home to her parents.

"Then let her come," Roff told the doctor and Mr. Vennum. "We'll be glad to let her come."

On February 11, "Mary Roff" moved to the Roff household. In the meanwhile, Dr. Stevens was learning more about Mary Lurancy's troubled past. It seemed that the child had led a normal life until about three years ago, when the troubling dreams began. One night she awoke, screaming, "There were persons in my room...and I felt their breath on my face!"

A few days later, she had another seizure, followed by another. She began to speak in "tongues," and complained that one particular spirit, Mary Roff, was trying to take over her body. The distressed family anxiously sought medical advice and were grateful when friends recommended Dr. Stevens, of Janesville, Wisconsin.

After "Mary Roff's" return to her family, she behaved exactly as if it were her own home—she recognized pieces of furniture, friends, photographs, clothes, and even the family pet. She was also quick to recall events from the past that only a member of the family could have known about.

Even when her real parents visited, Mary acted as if she hardly knew them.

Then, a few months later, Mary Lurancy Vennum's personality emerged. "What am I doing here?" she shouted, begging to be taken home to her parents immediately. A few minutes later, "Mary Roff" returned and took control. Over the course of the next several days, about a dozen similar transformations occurred.

On May 21, "Mary Roff," announced that she was going away, and gave the body back to Mary Lurancy Vennum. The departed spirit promised she would return some day, but not for a long, long time.

Back home in the Vennum household, Mary was able to get on with her normal life. Occasionally, she claimed that the other "Mary" would reappear briefly, but it seemed full possession was over. The girl would never again be racked by nightmares and eerie visits by uninvited guests from the spirit world.

Mary Lurancy Vennum's ordeal caught the attention of the press, and eventually swarms of scientists, mediums, clergymen, and others descended on the Vennum household to investigate. Dr. Richard Hodgson, a notoriously skeptical researcher of psychic phenomena, looked into the case and came to the conclusion that something incredible had indeed happened to the Vennum girl.

Exactly what that was, Hodgson was unable—or unwilling—to say. But troubling questions lingered: had the spirit of Mary Roff actually come back from the dead to invade the living Mary Lurance Vennum, as some serious researchers honestly believe?

Some investigators theorized the girl had not been visited by a ghost, but had somehow tapped into her own advanced psychic energy system to gather enough details about Mary Roff's past life to make her think she was the dead girl.

Had it all been nothing more than an brilliantly executed hoax?

The case of Mary Lurancy Vennum remains one of the great unexplained mysteries of psychic phenomena.

The House the Spirits Built

FOR NEARLY FOUR DECADES, Sarah L. Winchester went to sleep each night with the sound of saws and hammers echoing through her lonely old house on the outskirts of San Jose, California.

As long as there was noise, she could sleep. As long as the clatter and bang of men at work reverberated throughout the house, she could rest peacefully in her four-poster bed, knowing that she would live another day and that evil spirits would stay away another night.

Let the racket slack up for one moment and she was wide awake, shouting at the top of her lungs for the army of carpenters she employed night and day to get back to work.

That was how it had been for the melancholy old woman since 1884, the year she was widowed and left alone in an eight-room farmhouse in the Santa Clara Valley. Ever since, she had been obsessed with her peculiar destiny—to build and build and build in order that the sins of her late husband would be wiped clean and she would find peace once again.

Mrs. Winchester's torment had begun shortly after the death of her beloved husband, William Winchester, inventor of the famous Winchester repeating rifle that had won the Old West. In despair, she had turned to spiritualism for comfort. During a séance she was told that unless she spent all of her husband's money expanding and building her house she would never know peace.

Why such an unusual command from the spirit world?

"The souls of the victims killed by the rifles made by your husband—and there are thousands of them—seek revenge," the medium calmly replied. "Your life will be cursed unless you buy a house, enlarge it, and continue building it for the rest of your life."

As long as there was the sound of hammering in the house, Mrs. Winchester was told, she would not be troubled by the evil spirits. Her instructions were to add on to the house constantly—to expand, renovate and rebuild, day after day, night after night—to fill her sprawling home with a cacophony of rasping saws and clattering hammers and groaning pulley systems.

As long as she continued, the medium advised, she would be happy and never die.

So for the next thirty-eight years, until her death in 1922, Mrs. Winchester—one of the richest women in America—engaged hundreds of architects, designers, carpenters, and other workmen, many of whom worked in relays, to see the project through. Unremitting labor eventually wrought an eight-story house containing 750 rooms, 3 elevators, 6 kitchens, 40 bedrooms, 467 doors, 10,000 windows, 47 fireplaces, 40 stairways, 52 skylights, 6 safes, and a single shower.

No expense was spared. One door imported from Europe cost $800, while thousands were spent on several art glass windows. One room had four fireplaces and four hot-air radiators. In a climate where temperatures rarely came close to freezing, she had five separate central heating systems installed.

The nightmarish project was only beginning.

Convinced that spirits dwelled in cupboards, Sarah Winchester had them made in awkward shapes, sizes, and positions so the spirits within would be glad to leave. Eventually 2,000 cupboards were installed, some of them only an inch deep. Others connected adjoining rooms to the house.

For unknown reasons, several doors open only from one side, and others open into thin air. One set of stairs leads down to another set, then angles back up to the same story.

Another peculiar stairway has forty-four steps and turns seven corners—but rises a mere nine feet. Yet another leads directly up to the ceiling with no exit!

Remarkably, there are only two mirrors in the entire house—this apparently to spare whatever spirits inhabited the dwelling the embarrassment of not being able to see themselves.

Still not content with her grotesque creation, Mrs. Winchester ordered craftsmen to build a series of fake roofs and balconies to which there was no access. Pillars were placed upside down in several rooms. Miles and miles of wire ran throughout the house, connecting push-button communicating devices that not even the men who installed them understood how to work.

Through it all, the occult-inspired homeowner surrounded herself with gangs of servants and butlers. Most were easy to hire but, understandably, difficult to keep. As new chambers were added on, the household staff found it increasingly difficult to find their way about the maze of the house.

The Winchester house didn't go unnoticed by the outside world, either. The widow, who inherited her millionaire husband's entire fortune, was constantly bothered by outsiders who sought permission to look around the strange estate.

She always refused, saying she never received strangers, even when one caller happened to be the president of the United States, Theodore Roosevelt.

In 1922, the spirit-cursed millionairess felt chest pains but refused to accept the fact she was dying. Instead, she ordered her laborers to work harder and faster, to make even more noise than before in order to drive off the evil spirits coming to claim her soul. When she died a few days later, the entire house fell silent for the first time in nearly four decades as workmen laid down their tools as a mark of respect.

For the next sixteen years, the gloomy old house remained empty. Not a creature stirred within—no housemaid, no carpenter, no evil spirit. Silence reigned supreme.

Eventually permission was given to open the estate to the general public as a museum. To this day, however, there are some parts of the house that have never been fully explored. There are doorways and stairways leading to chambers yet unknown, entire wings that remain undisturbed in the silently shifting shadows.

The Ghost in the Library

LATE ONE NIGHT IN 1859, Dr. J. G. Cogswell was working alone at New York's Astor Library when he was suddenly startled by a noise a few aisles over. He thought there was nobody else in the library that time of night.

Curious, the doctor strolled over to investigate.

When he rounded the corner of a bookshelf, he was surprised to see an old man hunched over a table reading a book in the main gallery. There wasn't much light in the room—just enough for Cogswell to recognize something vaguely familiar about the frail stranger half-hidden in the shadows.

As he approached to inquire how the elderly gentleman had entered the locked building, the doctor couldn't shake the feeling that he somehow knew the man.

He couldn't quite put his finger on it.

The it hit him—the quaintly clad reader was his old friend, Washington Irving, the famous author who had helped found the library and often used its facilities.

But that was impossible. Washington Irving, the man who had given the world *The Legend of Sleepy Hollow, Rip Van Winkle,* and a dozen other literary masterpieces was *dead—* had been dead for several months. Cogswell had gone to his funeral!

Understandably, the doctor almost collapsed. By the time he recovered a few seconds later, the ghostly form of his friend had disappeared.

Shaken, Cogswell decided it was in his best interest not to tell anyone what he had seen. Who would believe him?

A few nights later, he was working late at the library again. The last group of visitors had left hours ago, and he was alone among the shifting shadows and creaking sounds of the musty old building. His reverie was suddenly interrupted by a strange popping noise—the same kind of noise he had heard the night the ghost of Washington Irving appeared.

He looked up, and sure enough, there stood the quivering form of his old friend again, white-haired head bent gracefully over a book. The ghost, half-hidden in the shadows, seemed oblivious to the doctor's presence. Determined to speak to it this time, Cogswell tiptoed over, so as not to frighten or startle the apparition.

Before he drew any closer, however, the ethereal presence started to fade—slowly at first, then faster and faster until there was nothing left but a few transparent patches of misty gray hovering over the book. They, too, finally disappeared, and the book crashed mysteriously to the floor.

When Cogswell later told some friends about what he had seen in the library, they solicitously encouraged him to go to the country for a few days of rest.

A couple of weeks later, a library user reported seeing a similar apparition. Then, in early 1860, Irving's own nephew, Pierre Irving, told friends that he had also seen his uncle's ghost, only this time, it was at the Irving home in Tarrytown, New York, instead of the library.

According to Pierre's account, he and his daughters were sitting in the living room when "the apparition suddenly walked through the parlor and entered the library" where Irving had done his writing. "Why, there's Uncle!" one of the girls is said to have exclaimed. They rushed into the library but found it empty.

In the years to come, numerous other sightings of Irving's ghost were reported, mostly at the Astor Library. Through the early 1860s, while the nation was engaged in a bloody

Civil War, New York newspapers frequently carried stories about the apparition alongside front page reports from the battlefield. In 1911, *The Nation* magazine ran an in-depth article on the Irving ghost.

The European press was also quick to pick up on the eerie story. As the first American author to gain international recognition, Irving had become a favorite among literary circles in England, France, and Germany. Some of his books and stories had hit the bestseller list in London, Paris, and Berlin long before they did in New York.

That's why so many fans, including Europeans, were fascinated by his own ghost story. This was the man, remember, who had written *The Legend of Sleepy Hollow*, a hair-raising tale about haunted woods, demons, and a headless horseman.

Drawing-room wisdom had it that Irving had returned from the dead to complete an unfinished novel he had been working on just before he died. There were also those who maintained that the ghost was only having fun, and that it was just like the prank-loving author to cause so much commotion even from the other side of the grave.

Irving himself would probably have gotten a big kick out of all the gossipy ghost stories circulated among New York's high society. It is ironic that the impish author, who didn't believe in the supernatural himself, was not only the author of America's first ghost story—"The Legend of Sleepy Hollow"—but would also become the subject of New York's most celebrated ghost tale.

Unearthly Incursions

Troubled Dreams and the Titanic

ON THE MORNING OF APRIL 10, 1912, an American woman named René Harris stood on the deck of the largest luxury oceanliner in the world and calmly watched the English shoreline grow fainter and fainter as the mighty vessel churned farther out to sea.

Suddenly a tall, handsome man whom she did not know approached her from across the crowded deck and abruptly asked, "Do you love life?"

A "black chill" swept over Mrs. Harris as she stared into the stranger's clouded eyes. When she replied that, yes, she did love life, the mysterious man said urgently, "Then get off this ship at Cherbourg, if we get that far. That's what I'm going to do."

His words would haunt the woman for the rest of her life.

The next morning, when the great ship anchored off Queenstown harbor to pick up the last of her transatlantic passengers, a sailor named John Coffey jumped ship. Like the stranger who spoke to Mrs. Harris, he, too, had a premonition of disaster.

Almost a week before, in a motel room in a small northern Illinois town, a well-known theatrical company manager named John Black awoke one night from a terrible dream. He sat straight up in bed and told some friends, "Folks, something terrible has happened! I saw a large ship sinking and hundreds of people being drowned. You will find it is true, because I saw the San Francisco earthquake and fire this same way at the time it happened."

All that week, beginning with Mr. Black's disturbing dream, scores of premonitions of disaster were being experienced by people on both sides of the Atlantic Ocean. Most of the paranormal revelations seemed to focus on death and icy waters and an incredibly large ship at sea.

Not much was made of it at the time, of course, because nothing had yet happened. Then, in the early morning hours of April 15, five days after Mrs. Harris' bizarre conversation with the stranger off the English coast, the ship on which she was sailing to New York slammed into a massive iceberg and sank, taking 1,503 people to their deaths in the icy North Atlantic. The ship was the *Titanic,* the mightiest and most magnificent ship in the world, the ship so well designed and built, people doubted that even God could take her down.

Down she went that cold spring morning, her proud and gleaming steel skin laid open to the weight and chill of the sea. When news of the disaster broke, it was as if a funeral pall had descended over the entire world.

There had been plenty of warnings—natural as well as supernatural. Only hours before her fateful collision with the mountain of jagged ice, the *Titanic* had received word from other ships that icebergs had been seen drifting in the *Titanic's* direction.

Captain Edwin J. Smith, under orders to make the fastest possible crossing—perhaps even to set a new record—ordered his crew to maintain their course full speed ahead.

By Sunday, the *Titanic* was in mid-Atlantic, still forging ahead at a steady twenty-two and one-half knots. Throughout the day, the wireless room picked up repeated messages about the hazards ahead. One vessel, the *Coronia,* notified her of "much ice" in the area. Some smaller vessels, including the French liner *Niagara,* had already been damaged by the ice and were limping out of harm's way back to port.

Meanwhile, the temperature of the sea around the *Titanic* dropped steadily. By midnight, it was well below freezing and still falling. Captain Smith pushed his ship onward, ignoring the growing dangers.

On the first-class deck, passengers were enjoying one of the most delightful evenings of the voyage. Dinner had been excellent—roast duck and English spring lamb, followed by endless rounds of champagne and brandy. In the background, conductor Wallace Hartley charmed his affluent audience with excerpts from "The Tales of Hoffman" and other popular melodies.

There, in their elaborate gowns and crisp tuxedos were some of the world's wealthiest people—Colonel John Jacob Astor, reportedly worth one hundred fifty million dollars; mining czar Benjamin Guggenheim; Isidor Straus, who acquired part of his forty million dollar fortune as co-founder of Macy's department stores; and Charles Melville Hays, president of the Grand Trunk Railroad.

All had gladly paid top dollar to be part of this historic crossing. Included in their $4,350 one-way fares were luxurious suites, each decorated in a different historical style, and all the food and drinks they could possibly hope to consume. On board the *Titanic*—at 882.5 feet, four times the length of a jumbo jet—was one of the most extravagant selections of wine in the world.

"She is," wrote one reporter taking part in the maiden voyage, "a floating Ritz Hotel."

Far below the ballroom floor, amid a maze of smoothly grinding gears and humming valves, the *Titanic's* fifty thousand horsepower engine propelled the doomed vessel steadily onward through the night.

At 11:40 p.m., a lookout in the crow's nest spotted an indefinite shape dead ahead. On this ship with every possible refinement, there were no binoculars in the crow's nest. A few seconds later, the sailor's right hand hit the alarm bell. Snatching the telephone connecting him to the bridge, he yelled, "Iceberg, right ahead!"

Instead of striking the iceberg head-on—which might have kept her afloat—the *Titanic* veered to starboard, exposing her thin steel hull to the jagged mountain of ice looming out of the darkness. The collision peeled the ship's skin back as if with a can opener.

Almost immediately, walls of water flooded the engine rooms and drowned several sailors there. Panic set in among some of the crew members at the lower levels. Higher up, oblivious to the horror unfolding in the ship's bowels, the dancing and feasting continued a brief while longer.

Up on the bridge, the situation was grim. Captain Smith, clad in a formal white uniform, reacted to the news with the detached calm of a condemned man. The telephone rang constantly. Terrified officers awaited instructions.

Finally, the seasoned captain realized he had no choice but to order the ship abandoned. Water was coming in too fast. The *Titanic* was beginning to list dangerously. It was only a matter of time until the ship's stern pitched skyward in a grotesque kick, and the vessel slid beneath the freezing dark waters of the Atlantic.

Since there weren't enough lifeboats to accommodate all the passengers, the captain ordered women and children off first. Any remaining boats would be taken by the crippled and elderly, but he and his 800-man crew would remain with the *Titanic*.

As the lifeboats were lowered and pulled away from the dying ship, Wallace Hartley and his musicians bravely struck up a medley of ragtime favorites. Contrary to legend, they did not play "Nearer My God to Thee" but another Episcopal tune called "Autumn."

At exactly 2:20 a.m., the *Titanic's* stern finally reared out of the sea like a monstrous whale, and she slid bow-first into the inky waters. Down with her went Hartley and his gallant musicians, Captain Smith and his crew, and hundreds of other brave men and women who had yielded their seats on the limited number of lifeboats.

All told, 1,503 lives were lost that night, including 533 men, women, and children from tourist class and 120 from the first-class section. The wonder is that so many survived, considering the frigid weather and the long wait until rescue boats arrived.

Could the disaster have been avoided? Quite a few experts believe it could have, had officials only heeded the flood of premonitions the week before. Ian Stevenson, the well-known professor of parapsychology at the University of Virginia, says the sinking of the *Titanic* was accompanied by more paranormal experiences than any other sea disaster on record. He doesn't know why, but theorizes that the "shock" of the event might have contributed in some unknown way.

"I suggest that the very unexpectedness of the sinking of the *Titanic* may have generated an emotional shock not present in disasters that are less surprising, such as the sinking of the *Lusitania* and most military battleships" the scientist explained.

In the first place, he noted, nobody believed the ship *could* sink. That included its builders, financiers, crewmen, passengers, and the general public. Even Captain Smith, in the face of imminent danger, refused to accept the fact that something as mundane as an iceberg could wreck his gleaming new ship.

Could there have been some kind of as yet unexplained link between the multitude of premonitions of disaster and the unswerving conviction that the fabulous *Titanic* was unsinkable?

Stevenson published several corroborated reports which suggest that nineteen people had extrasensory awareness of the sinking of the *Titanic*—ten of whom seemed to have knowledge of the calamity in advance. Had enough of these premonitions been made public, Stevenson theorizes, the outcome of the *Titanic*'s maiden voyage might have been different.

The Triangle of Lost Souls

OF ALL THE WORLD'S MYSTERIES, none has bedeviled the experts more than the Bermuda Triangle, a picturesque, seemingly ordinary and peaceful patch of Atlantic Ocean stretching eastward from Florida and Puerto Rico to Bermuda.

But as any tabloid junkie knows, there is more to this lovely region than meets the eye—*much* more, when you consider the fact that at least one thousand people and an estimated one hundred ships and aircraft have vanished in the Triangle in the past four decades alone.

Beneath these calm subtropical waters, or above in the sun-splashed skies, some unknown force seems to be at work, gobbling up ships and planes and people at an alarming rate. They sound like good old *gotcha!* scenes from a poorly scripted grade-B flick—ships sucked into oblivion as if by magic, airplanes soaring off course and out of this world through a mysterious hole in the sky, eerie "blue holes" and flashing undersea lights—but they're real, if you accept any one of a number of theories currently being bandied about by the "experts."

Even by-the-book governmental agencies such as the Federal Aviation Administration admit that there are "special problems" associated with flying in the area. The U.S. Coast Guard regards the Triangle as one of the most dangerous maritime regions on earth.

A slightly more cautious attitude is taken by the Institute of Oceanography in London, where a spokesman said, "We have no reason to believe that there is anything in that part of the ocean that is any different from other parts of the Atlantic. I personally tend to support the natural causes explanations...but you never know, do you?"

It should be pointed out that most scientists and hard-nosed governmental and military authorities do insist that most accidents can be attributed to such mundane factors as weather, inexperience in over-ocean flying, and inadequate navigation equipment.

Still, the controversy rages on, year after year, with all sides squared toward the middle.

What exactly is the Bermuda Triangle, how did it get its name, and why all the fuss over a bit of sub-tropical sea?

Christopher Columbus was probably the first person on record to have noticed something wrong about the waters in the Triangle. In his logbook, he wrote about flaming balls of fire whizzing through powder-blue skies and "glowing streaks of white on the surface"—an observation echoed five centuries later when U.S. astronauts orbiting the earth described "mysterious patches of light and foam" off Bermuda.

It wasn't until 1945, however, that the world's attention was focused on the mysterious realm. In December of that year, an entire squadron of Navy bombers vanished without a trace somewhere off the coast of Florida.

Though ships have been involved in mysterious calamities within the Bermuda Triangle for centuries, it was the disappearance of Flight 19 along with twenty-seven crewmen that rekindled rumors about the region. Flight 19, based at the Fort Lauderdale, Florida, Naval Air Station, was on a routine training mission when the lead pilot radioed that he was "lost," and gave the following cryptic message: "Everything is wrong. We can't be sure of any direction. Even the ocean doesn't look as it should."

Despite a massive air-sea rescue operation involving three hundred planes, four destroyers, several submarines, and hundreds of boats and ships, no trace of Flight 19 was ever found.

One clue to the squadron's fate was revealed in a broadcast picked up by an amateur radio operator. "Don't come after me," the flight leader told base. "They look like they are from outer space." Those exact words were confirmed in an official transcript of the messages between the flight and base.

Eighteen months after the Flight 19 tragedy, the Triangle sucked another victim from the skies when a U.S. Army Superfort disappeared a hundred miles off Bermuda without having signaled any hint of trouble. Again, an immediate search of a hundred thousand square miles of sea failed to turn up a single piece of wreckage.

A few years later, a DC-3 with thirty-six people aboard apparently "evaporated" within clear sight of Miami. "We are approaching the field only fifty miles to the south," the pilot told the control tower. "We can see the lights of Miami now. All's well. Will stand by for landing instructions."

All was not well. The plane vanished from the radar screen a few seconds later and was never seen or heard from again. Yet the spot where the aircraft supposedly went down was over the Florida Keys, where clear waters only twenty feet deep should have made the DC-3 clearly visible.

Tragedy struck again in October 1954, when an American U.S. Navy Super Constellation carrying forty-two people disappeared. No trace of the aircraft was ever found.

While plane after plane was "de-materializing," more bizarre evidence was piling up from pilots who had survived the power of the Triangle. One of the most unusual stories was given by the pilot of a Pan-American DC-6, who said he had to swerve violently to avoid colliding with a "mysterious luminous object" off the coast of Florida.

The Triangle's prodigious plane-eating seems not to reduce its appetite for ships. So many vessels have gone down in the region over the years under peculiar circumstances, it would be impossible to list them all here. The tale of the *Ellen Austin*, however, deserves special mention.

In 1881, the crew of the *Ellen Austin* sighted a schooner drifting off the coast of Bermuda. Intrigued, the captain ordered his ship to draw near, then dispatched some crew-men aboard to investigate. They found plenty of food and a handsome cargo of mahogany—but no sign of life anywhere. There was no indication of struggle, and everything appeared to be in place, including all lifeboats.

The captain of the *Ellen Austin* ordered a hand-picked crew to sail the stranded vessel with its valuable load on into port. Before long, however, a storm blew up and the two ships lost contact with each other.

Two days later, the two ships came together again. Everything looked fine—except that the newly-installed crew had disappeared! The captain of the *Ellen Austin* once again stationed a fresh crew aboard the mysterious ship—this time all volunteers.

As before, the ships sailed on together until another storm drove them apart. The next day, the men of the *Ellen Austin* waited patiently for a rendezvous with the schooner, but they would never see the mysterious ship again. It had vanished—this time for good—with all hands on board.

Speculation abounds about the region's alleged connection with extra-terrestrial beings, time warps, the lost continent of Atlantis, even the supernatural. As radical as some of those suggestions sound, investigators are hard put to come up with alternative explanations.

How can so many airplanes and ships—some within clear sight of shore—suddenly and inexplicably disappear without leaving behind any wreckage or debris, not even a tell-tale oil slick? How can there be so many losses with no survivors, no logs, no tapes, and few radio messages beamed ashore that might shed light on what happened? How in this age of improved radio communications can so many modern ships and jet aircraft equipped with high-tech equipment and highly trained crewmen simply disappear?

While skeptics point to purely natural causes—human error, mechanical breakdown, Gulf Stream currents, and sudden, violent changes in the weather—a growing number of people, scientists and journalists included, insist there is probably more to the story than is being told.

Much of the information that has emerged in recent years seems to confirm what legions of Triangle watchers already knew: that something dark and troubling and potentially dangerous stalks the region, and that it's high time the government launched a serious, full-scale investigation.

The Mysterious Night Flyers

EARLY ONE EVENING IN THE spring of the year, Robert Lowen, of Evanston, Illinois, was out walking his dog when he looked up and saw a strange light moving slowly across the sky.

Intrigued, Lowen ran inside the house and grabbed his field glasses. He had heard about such lights and was determined to get a good look at the phenomenon before it disappeared.

He was in luck. Not only was the light still visible when he got back outside, there seemed to be others as well—all strung together, like searchlights emanating from a single object.

Lowen watched the dazzling display of lights for about ten minutes before it disappeared. He went to bed that night convinced he had seen something truly extraordinary.

Apparently thousands of other people had seen something extraordinary that night as well, for the next day the offices of the *Chicago Tribune* were crowded with excited people demanding an investigation. Convinced that the story was legitimate, the paper ran a front-page article about the sighting.

The next day more reports of sightings came in, so the newspaper ran another story. Then another and another. In the days and weeks that followed, hundreds of persons living in the Chicago area came forward with still more stories about strange flashing lights in the night skies.

By the end of the month, it seemed that just about everybody in the Chicago area had seen the mysterious airship at least once. Typical of the accounts published in the newspaper was the following:

"At several points, the moving wonder was observed by persons equipped with small telescopes or powerful field glasses, and those persons claim to have described the outlines of a structure bearing the lights."

The article went on to report that "the consensus of judgment...is that the main body of the night flyer was about seventy feet in length, of slender proportions and fragile construction. To this body, it is reported, were attached the movable headlight and other lights described. A few observers claim that they also saw, a short distance above the body, lateral structures, resembling wings or sails."

Strange sightings of unexplained aerial phenomena are nothing new in the country. Since the late 1940s, in fact, newspapers and magazines around the world have published countless articles about strange flashing lights in the sky, flying saucers, and other unidentified flying objects (UFOs). It would be impossible to count the number of documentaries and full-length feature films that have been presented on the subject, from the B flicks of the 1950s to modern classics such as "E.T."

What makes Robert Lowen's account so unusual, however, is the fact it occurred not in the 1940s or 1950s, or even the 1990s, but in April, 1897—a full seven years before the Wright brothers managed to get their flying machine off the ground. Except for a few inventors, scientists, and science-fiction fans, few people had ever heard of an airship, much less one with flashing lights that appeared and disappeared at will.

But that year, from the fall of 1896 through the spring of 1897, tens of thousands of Americans from California to West Virginia watched such mysterious airships whirl and twinkle overhead. Sketches and photographs were made by a few observers, some of which were published in newspapers and magazines.

Understandably, the "invasion" of airships alarmed a lot of people—especially when they began hovering over scores of large cities such as Sacramento, Omaha, and Chicago. Typical of those who reacted fearfully to the sightings was Lowen himself, who gave the following account to the Chicago Tribune:

"I was able to discern four lights a short distance apart and moving in unison," he was quoted. "The first was a bright white light and appeared to be operated like a searchlight. Behind it was a green light and further to the rear were green and white lights strung together."

Predictably, the national press was quick to capitalize on the phenomenon. Sensational stories filled the major newspapers and magazines, boosting newsstand sales and subscriptions. Papers as far away as England, France, and Germany also featured stories about the American sightings, as well as accounts by their own European countrymen.

Each account seemed wilder and more frightening than the previous one. Some witnesses described terrifying encounters with bizarre creatures who descended from the airships and aimed "rays of light" at them. There were a couple of incidents apparently involving abduction.

Then, almost as suddenly as they had started, the mysterious sightings ended—at least the newspapers were publishing fewer and fewer stories about them. By the time the Wright brothers launched their dramatic flight at Kitty Hawk, just about everybody had forgotten about the mysterious airships.

Nobody knows why all the hoopla suddenly died down. Whatever the reason, one of the greatest mysteries of the nineteenth century simply went away unsolved.

What caused all the excitement in the first place? One popular theory at the time was that an unknown inventor had built a "lighter-than-air" ship and was secretly testing the aircraft. Investigators failed to find the elusive inventor, even though a few people believed then—as now—that the government was somehow behind the experiment. (The same people who accept this are usually the same ones who argue that the government has secretly resumed its search for UFOs and has even made contact with extraterrestrial beings.)

There were deliberate hoaxes as well. Several people were caught releasing hot-air balloons rigged with lights. Newspapers—even the reputable ones—were not above sensationalizing the news now and then in order to sell papers. In fact, hoaxes were considered legitimate journalism in some editorial circles at the end of the nineteenth century.

One source even suggested that railroad telegraph operators were engaged in a conspiracy to spread airship stories. Just why, no one knows.

What *is* known is that science-fiction stories had become extremely popular in those days, and many of the stories featured quaint mechanical inventions, air travel, and even time travel.

Though people stopped talking about them, memories of the airships lingered past the turn of the century. It wouldn't be until almost half a century later—the 1950s—that the world would once again be rocked by sightings of unidentified flying objects.

Lights Over Troubled Water

IT WAS A TYPICAL JANUARY evening along the California coast—velvet sky, shimmering waves, and the mouth-watering aroma of T-bones sizzling over an open flame.

There was nothing George Clemens liked better than cooking out, especially on crisp wintry nights by the seashore. As mayor of Monterey, though, he rarely found the time anymore. On this night, January 29, 1965, he was determined to *make* time; even punks on Harleys couldn't have dragged him away from his favorite family pastime.

Everything was going fine until something out over the water caught his attention. It was like a spark, a very bright spark, that lit up the sky for a couple of seconds, then blinked out.

At once, it was back again, wheeling and soaring, a dazzling display of bright colors. This time, other family members saw it. For several seconds, the entire Clemens clan watched spellbound as the peculiar light performed "aerial acrobatics" in the pitch-black sky.

According to the mayor's account published in the local newspaper the next day, the object "hovered for a while, then shot straight up at a high speed for about five hundred feet, then faded and dropped down and hovered again."

After hovering for several more seconds, the mysterious light plunged into the dark waters and disappeared.

As it turned out, a local pilot had spotted a similar light the same night, but a Coast Guard investigation found nothing. The case was dropped.

Earlier that month, an Oregon newspaper had reported a similar incident in which Mrs. Paul Zimmerman Gearhart and her two sons had watched a triangular mass of lights "suddenly plunge into the sea some miles offshore" near Tillamook Head, leaving behind two trails of fire.

Seven months later, on August 3, the Barking Sand tracking station of Kauai Island, Hawaii, observed a "rocket-type object" that crashed into the ocean about ten miles south of the island. Other islanders who had witnessed the phenomena claimed the object fell "like a rock." United Air Lines pilot L. L. Jones described it as yellow-green, with an "overgrown falling star" appearance.

In December, Mrs. Irwin Cohen of San Pedro, California, said she and her son took pictures of a glowing red-orange object that went down nose-first into the ocean. Mrs. Cohen said steam rose from the object as it struck the water, leading her to suspect it was some kind of Navy missile.

Glowing balls of fire crashing into the sea, greenish-yellow lights rising over the ocean and blazing across the night skies, unusual patterns of smoke trailing behind objects entering the water at great speeds—the sightings have the ocean in common.

That doesn't surprise a lot of UFO watchers who have insisted for years on a connection between alien spacecraft and the watery depths around the globe. A growing number of observers have commented on the high percentage of UFO sightings in the vicinity of lakes, rivers, and open seas. By some estimates, at least half of all sightings have occurred in or over water—a fact that can't be ignored, according to Ivan R. Sanderson, a well-known scientist and naturalist currently engaged in the esoteric study of phenomena linked to UFOs.

Citing hundreds of reliable reports—both historic and recent—Sanderson and his small team of co-researchers maintain that something strange is going on beneath the dark, still waters of our world's lakes, rivers, and oceans.

"Men live on land—only about a quarter of the earth's surface," Sanderson notes in his study of the subject, *Invisible Residents*, considered by some to be the definitive sourcebook about underwater alien activity. "In recent years we have begun to explore the space above our planet—but what of the seventy-five percent of earth that lies beneath water?"

Sanderson suggests that we have been ignoring "the mountain of evidence that something strange is happening down there."

Sanderson believes there is a government conspiracy to cover up the truth about the mysterious water-related goings-on. He claims that high-ranking members of the government and the military have long known about the coming and going of extraterrestrial life at the bottom of the sea, but choose to keep a lid on it for fear the public might panic.

"There is nothing that officialdom dreads more than having to admit that it doesn't know what is going on, or what everything or anything is all about, and, more specifically, having to admit that they have no real answers or remedies."

The fact is, nobody seems to know what is going on, even though reports of UAOs (a Sanderson-inspired acronym for "unidentified aerial object") continue to make news every year. While a fair number of such sightings can easily be dismissed as meteorological phenomena, weather balloon activity, and falling stars, experts and eyewitnesses have failed to account for most.

For example, on the night of April 1, 1952, an object resembling an airplane fell into the Gulf of Mexico some two hundred miles south of Lake Charles, Louisiana. The captain of the *S.S. Esso Bermuda* dutifully reported the crash to the Coast Guard, but a search failed to turn up anything unusual in the area.

In March, 1954, San Francisco Bay area police stations were swamped with calls reporting that "hundreds of boats" were gathering offshore. When the Coast Guard chugged out to investigate, it found nothing, although other callers insisted that hundreds of red and orange lights had been spotted "bobbing in the ocean" just south of Golden Gate Park.

In late summer of 1954, the *Groote Beer*, a Dutch-registered container vessel, arrived in New York with a strange story. The captain, a grizzled mariner named Jan P. Boshoff, swore that he watched a "strange, flat, moonlike object rise out of the ocean." The ship's third officer, Cornelius Kooey, reported that the grayish-colored object was clocked at a high rate of speed.

A few months later the Navy Hydrographic Office reported that crewmen aboard the American tanker *Dynafuel*, sailing the Gulf of Mexico not far from New Orleans, saw smoke on the water. "The smoke appeared to come from under water and resembled smoke from bombs dropped during target practice," the ship's captain noted in his official report.

Other examples...

—July 22, 1955. Witnesses in Santa Maria, California, are frightened when they see a "long, silvery object emerge from the water."

—February, 1955. Annabell Culverwell of Jerome, Arizona, vacationing at Ocean Beach, California, sees a "hugh geyser of water with the rear end of what looked like a space ship protruding from the top...The geyser subsided [and] at the place where the geyser disappeared was a ring of what looked like wooly clouds."

—June 22, 1957. Two policemen in Rye, New York, watch a large object with two white lights and one red light plunge into Long Island Sound.

—August 20, 1964. Two boys, Pat and Cliff Irwin of Richland, Washington, tell the Coast Guard that a red-and-white plane crashed in the sea off Oysterville, leaving a red-and-white smoke trail. The Coast Guard checked the report, but found nothing; no planes were missing.

—March 13, 1958. Navy pilots flying fifty miles north of San Francisco spot an "undersea object" which refused to identify itself.

—July, 1961. *The Ruby H*, a 67-foot shrimp boat owned by Ira Pete of Alaska, "hooked something" that ripped the vessel's stern off while cruising off Port Aransas in the Gulf of Mexico.

—August 9, 1963. A 90-foot dragger fishing off Portland, Maine, nearly capsizes when an unidentified underwater object becomes entangled in her nets. The Navy said no subs were in the area at the time.

—February 5, 1964. A 105-foot converted PT boat, the *Hattie D.*, strikes an unidentified object twenty-five miles off Cape Mendocino, California, and sinks. Said the captain: "We struck an unseen object. It was not a log. It was like metal…. It definitely was a strange object."

—July 5, 1965. While conducting one-man submarine operations off Fort Pierce, Florida, Dr. Dmitri Rebikoff observes a "pear-shaped object…" At first he thought it was a shark, but "its direction and speed were too constant. It may have been running on a robot pilot. We received no signal from it and therefore do not know what it was."

—September 27, 1966. Two divers from the Naval Ordinance Laboratory Test Facility discover a rocket-like object in forty feet of water off the coast of Miami.

Something odd and fascinating seems to be going on down below, but what is it? Even if we accept only a fraction of the documented cases—cases presented by veteran mariners, airline pilots, police officers, and other creditable people— why aren't more experts looking into it? Where is *Time* magazine? NBC Nightly News? Even "A Current Affair"?

Could it be that a lot of sensible people, journalists included, are reluctant to step forward and probe or talk for fear of being ridiculed? That makes sense, considering the fallout that most UFO watchers get when they go on record with a report. Remember Jimmy Carter's famous flying saucer?

Bibliography

Adler, Bill, ed. *UFOs*. New York: Dell Publishing, 1967.

American Heritage Books. *Mysteries of the Past*. New York: American Heritage Books, 1977.

Arens, W. *The Man-Eating Myth*. New York: Oxford University Press, 1984.

Baity, Elizabeth Chesley. *America Before Man*. New York: Viking Press, 1959.

Benwell, Gwen, and Arthur Waugh. *Sea Enchantress*. New York: The Citadel Press, 1965.

Berlitz, Charles. *The Bermuda Triangle*. New York: Doubleday & Company, 1974.

Bernstein, Morey. *The Search for Bridey Murphy*. New York: Doubleday & Company, 1956.

Blum, John M. *The National Experience*. New York: Harcourt Brace Jovanovich, 1973.

Bolton, Herbert E., ed. *Arrendondo's Historical Proof of Spain's Title to Georgia*. Berkeley: University of California Press, 1925.

Botkin, B.A. *A Treasury of American Folklore*. New York: Bonanza Books, 1967.

Bray, Warwick M., and Earl H. Swanson. *The New World*. New York: E.P. Dutton, 1976.

Bremer, Francis J. *The Puritan Experiment*. New York: St. Martin's Press, 1976.

Bushnell, Geoffrey Hext Sutherland. *The First Americans*. New York: McGraw-Hill, 1975.

Carrington, Richard. *Mermaids and Mastodons.* New York: Rinehart & Company, Inc., 1957.

Carter, Hodding. *Doomed Road to Empire: The Spanish Trail of Conquest.* New York: McGraw-Hill, 1963.

Ceram, C.W. *The First American.* New York: Harcourt Brace Jovanovich, 1971.

Clark, Arthur C. *Arthur C. Clark's Mysterious World.* New York: A. & W. Publishers, 1980.

Cottrell, Leonard. *Lost Worlds.* New York: Dell Publishing, 1962.

Crane, Verner W. *The Southern Frontier.* New York: W.W. Norton and Company, 1981.

von Daniken, Erich. *Miracles of the Gods.* New York: Dell Publishing, 1975.

Davis, Nigel. *Voyages to the New World.* New York: William Morrow and Company, 1979.

Day, A. Grove. *Coronado's Quest.* Los Angeles: University of California Press, 1964.

Del Ray, Lester. *The Mysterious Earth.* New York: Chilton Company, 1961.

de Camp, L. Sprague. *Lost Continents.* New York: Dover Publications, 1970.

_____, and Willy Ley. *Lands Beyond.* New York: Rinehart & Company, 1952.

DeVoto, Bernard. *The Course of Empire.* Boston: Houghton Mifflin Company, 1952.

Erdoes, Richard, and Alfonso Ortiz. *American Indian Myths and Legends.* New York: Pantheon Books, 1984.

Fell, Barry. *America, B.C.* New York: Demeter Press, 1977.

Gerster, Patrick, and Nicholas Cards. *Myth in American History.* Encino, California: Glencoe Press, 1977.

Goodman, Jeffrey. *American Genesis.* New York: Summit Books, 1981.

Grumley, Michael. *There Are Giants in the Earth.* New York: Doubleday & Company, 1974.

Hansen, Chadwick. *Witchcraft at Salem.* New York: George Braziller, 1969.

184

Heuvelmans, Bernard. *In the Wake of Sea Serpents.* New York: Hill and Wang, 1969.

Hill, Douglas, and Pat Williams. *The Supernatural.* New York: Signet Books, 1965.

Hordern, Nicholas. *The Conquest of North America.* New York: Doubleday & Company, 1973.

Hudson, Charles. *The Southeastern Indians.* Knoxville: University of Tennessee Press, 1976.

Jacob, Kathryn Allamong. "She Couldn't Have Done It." American Heritage 29 (February/March, 1978).

Jenkinson, Michael. *Beasts Beyond the Fire.* New York: E.P. Dutton, 1980.

Jennings, Jesse D., and Edward Norbeck. *Prehistoric Man in the New World.* Chicago: The University of Chicago Press, 1964.

King, Edward. *The Great South.* Baton Rouge: Louisiana State University, 1970.

Kirkpatrick, F.A. *The Spanish Conquistadores.* New York: World Publishing, 1971.

Kusche, Lawrence David. *The Bermuda Triangle Mystery— Solved.* New York: Harper & Row, 1975.

Lupols, Harry Forrest. *The Forgotten People: The Woodland Erie.* Hicksville, New York: Exposition Press, 1975.

Mahan, Joseph. *The Secret: America in World History Before Columbus.* Acworth, Georgia: Star Printing Co., 1985.

Maple, Eric. *The Dark World of Witches.* New York: Castle Books, 1970.

Meggers, Betty J. *Prehistoric America.* Chicago: Aldine Publishing Company, 1973.

Morison, Samuel Eliot. *The European Discovery of America: the Northern Voyages.* New York: Oxford University Press, 1974.

_____. *The European Discovery of America: The Southern Voyages.* New York: Oxford University Press, 1974.

Ogburn, Charlton. *The Southern Appalachians.* New York: William Morrow & Company, 1975.

Phillips, Perrott, ed. *Out of This World: The Illustrated Library of the Bizarre and Extraordinary.* New York: Columbia House, 1978.

Reader's Digest. *American Folklore and Legend.* Pleasantville, New York: Reader's Digest Associates, 1978.

_____. *Mysteries of the Unexplained.* Pleasantville, New York: Reader's Digest Books, 1977.

_____. *Mysteries of the Ancient Americas: The New World Before Columbus.* Pleasantville, New York: Reader's Digest Books, 1986.

_____. *Strange Stories, Amazing Facts.* Pleasantville, New York: Reader's Digest Books

Ribeiro, Darcy. *The Americas and Civilization.* New York: E.P. Dutton, 1972.

Riegel, Robert E., and Robert G. Athearn. *America Moves West.* Hinsdale, Illinois: The Dryden Press, Inc., 1971.

Sanders, Ronald. *Lost Tribes and Promised Lands.* Boston: Little, Brown and Company, 1946.

Sanderson, Ivan T. *Invisible Residents.* New York: The World Publishing Company, 1982.

Silverberg, Robert. *Frontiers in Archaeology.* New York: Chilton Book Company, 1968.

_____. *The Morning of Mankind.* New York: New York Graphic Society Publishers, Inc., 1967.

Smith, Page. *A New Age Now Begins.* New York: McGraw-Hill, 1976.

Steibing, William H. Jr. *Ancient Astronauts, Cosmic Collisions.* New York: Prometheus Books, 1984.

Sweeney, James B. *A Pictorial History of Sea Monsters.* New York: Bonanza Books, 1972.

Thorndike, Joseph, ed. *Mysteries of the Deep.* New York: American Heritage Publishing Company, 1980.

Time-Life Books. *Mystic Places.* Alexandria, Virginia: Time-Life Books, 1987.

Vaughan, Alden. *Incredible Coincidences: The Baffling World of Synchronicity.* New York: J.B. Lippincott, 1979.

Verrill, A. Hyatt. *Strange Prehistoric Animals and Their Stories.* Boston: L.C. Page & Company, 1954.

_____. *The Strange Story of Our Earth*. Boston: L.C. Page & Company, 1952.

Walker, Hugh. *Tennessee Tales*. Nashville: Aurora Publishers, 1970.

Watson, Don. *Indians of the Mesa Verde*. Mesa Verde National Park, ColoradoL Mesa Verde Museum Association. 1961.

Willey, Gordon R., and Jeremy A. Sabloff. *A History of American Archaeology*. San Francisco: W.H. Freeman, 1974.

Wilmsen, Edwin N. *Lindenmier: A Pleistocene Hunting Society*. New York: Harper & Row, 1974.

Wormington, H.M. *Ancient Man in North American*. Denver: The Denver Museum of Natural History, undated.

Index of Place Names

E. Randall Floyd lives in Augusta, Georgia, where he teaches history at Augusta College. His syndicated column appears weekly in more than seventy-seven newspapers. He has written two books—Great Southern Mysteries and More Great Southern Mysteries—and holds advanced degrees in history and modern foreign languages, and worked as a foreign correspondent for United Press International. His wife, Anne Shelander Floyd, is a historic preservation planner and museum studies consultant.